# TREASON in the ROCKIES

# TREASON in the ROCKIES

## NAZI SYMPATHIZER DALE MAPLE'S POW ESCAPE PLOT

PAUL N. HERBERT

Foreword by Flint Whitlock

THE History PRESS

Published by The History Press
Charleston, SC
www.historypress.net



*Front cover, bottom left*: Courtesy of Library of Congress, Prints and Photographs Division, FSA/OWI Collection, LC-USW33-022634-D.

First published 2016

Manufactured in the United States

ISBN 978.1.46713.537.5

Library of Congress Control Number: 2016945801

*To Artie Crisp and J. Banks Smither from The History Press for their expertise and support. It's a joy working with people like them who toil mightily to help turn fascinating topics of history into highly readable books.*

# Contents

# Foreword

There are millions of stories that came out of World War II, but Paul Herbert's story of U.S. Army private Dale H. Maple is one of the strangest, most fascinating and least known.

Dale Maple was a brilliant, Harvard-educated soldier from California fluent in twenty languages but who had an odd admiration for Nazi Germany. In the late 1930s, he was a member of the school's German Club, had once shown up at a campus Halloween party dressed as Hitler and had gotten kicked out of the school's ROTC program for espousing pro-Nazi views. When war broke out, however, Maple enlisted in the army, not waiting to be drafted. His pro-German sympathies soon came to the fore.

Eventually, he was assigned to the 620th Engineer General Service Company—a unit primarily made up of disgruntled American soldiers suspected of disloyalty. The 620th was sent from Fort Meade, South Dakota, to Camp Hale, Colorado—an army post high in the Rocky Mountains where America's elite mountain soldiers were being trained.

Somehow, through someone's obvious oversight, the 620th happened to be billeted adjacent to a German prisoner-of-war enclosure in the camp. (There were hundreds of POW camps inside the United States during the war holding some 400,000 German, Italian and Japanese prisoners.) It was here that Maple befriended a few of the 250 German prisoners, former members of Erwin Rommel's famed Afrika Korps who had been captured in North Africa.

Fraternizing with prisoners is something prohibited by army regulations, a fact that did not trouble the misguided Maple. His friendship with two of them soon resulted in an escape plot that involved Maple buying a used car and a pistol, somehow getting the two men out of the prisoner enclosure, leaving the camp and driving the three of them south, through New Mexico and toward the Mexican border. There the hastily conceived plan was for the trio to be spirited out of the country by German agents and across the Atlantic to the Fatherland. Running out of gas a few miles short of the border, the trio walked across the line but were soon picked up by Mexican authorities, returned to the United States and handed over to the FBI.

Maple, in addition to helping the prisoners escape, had become a traitor and a deserter. Both charges carried a possible death sentence, which, after a court-martial in which Maple was found guilty, was imposed. President Roosevelt later commuted the sentence to life imprisonment.

The extent of the author's research is evident throughout, and he has produced not only a readable, finely detailed account of Maple's treasonous activities but also a larger portrait of the practically unknown story of enemy combatants being held in the United States, the conditions of their incarceration, and their many attempts to escape. Paul Herbert is to be commended for bringing to light this intriguing wartime tale that has been, until now, allowed to slip through the radar of history.

Flint Whitlock
Editor, *WWII Quarterly* magazine
Coauthor of *Soldiers on Skis: A Pictorial Memoir of the 10th Mountain Division*

# Preface

This book is about an obscure event in American history. A few magazine articles have been written about it, and it's on *Wikipedia*. The U.S. Army retains voluminous court-martial files, so any researcher can read the original documents. The story's obscurity results partially from the controversy during World War II surrounding its two key elements, the first of which concerns the existence of hundreds of camps here in the United States that held almost half a million foreign soldiers. During the war, the army didn't publicize the camps. Even to this day, to the general population, the existence of the camps remains largely unknown or shrouded in confusion.

The second element causing obscurity concerns the existence of army "special organizations" during World War II. These organizations contained hundreds of American soldiers that the army considered disloyal. The soldiers weren't advised they were considered disloyal or told how that determination was arrived at or by whom. They didn't have any kind of hearing to defend themselves or make their cases. Soldiers paid a pretty steep personal and career price once they were labeled disloyal. Certainly, the actions of many earned their placement in the camps. But this topic is dangerous stuff, fraught with legal and moral issues. It's no wonder the army didn't publicize it.

# Acknowledgements

My thanks to Flint Whitlock for writing the foreword; Sarah Gilmor, Melissa VanOtterloo, Kirby Stokes and Aaron Marcus of the History Colorado Center; Keli Schmid at the Tenth Mountain Division Resource Center of the Denver Public Library; Diane Bell of the *San Diego Union-Tribune*; Captain Manion Long of the Doña Ana, New Mexico Sheriff's Department; Artie Crisp, J. Banks Smither, Candice Lawrence and Julia Turner from The History Press; Ron Owens; Delona Bryce for sharing her memories of her grandfather; Mike Kaszuba at the El Cajon Historical Society; Beth Benko for helping with research; independent historian Ricky Robertson; Audrey Kalivoda and Susie Haver of the Camp Concordia Preservation Society; Jennifer Orrigo Charles of Colorado Preservation Inc.; Matthew Rector and Joseph Yates for helping with the photo at the Cultural Resources Office at Fort Knox; Itzel Gonzalez of the San Diego High School Alumni Association; Cathy Lazarus for the Camp Hearne photos; Rachel Mosman of the Oklahoma Historical Society; Tom Mudugno of the Goleta History Center, Dale Sauter and Jennifer Joyner of East Carolina University; and Christy Calhoun of the Mississippi Armed Forces Museum.

# Introduction

Among the hundreds of German soldiers confined to the prisoner of war stockade at Camp Hale, Colorado, during the last weekend of January 1944, one man didn't belong. He appeared to fit in, in the sense that he wore the standard prison garb—the "PW" stenciled in white on his blue clothes. But he wasn't a German prisoner. He wasn't a prisoner at all. He had never been to Germany and, in fact, had never traveled overseas and had no known German heritage. He traced his family roots for generations to Illinois, New York and Kentucky. This ersatz prisoner of war was actually a private in the U.S. Army. He knew the rules against fraternizing with enemy prisoners, but he nevertheless surreptitiously entered the prison camp, hidden on a truck. Not much else is known about his weekend among the throng of prisoners or how he inconspicuously left their lair and returned to the U.S. Army camp without drawing unwanted attention.

In the prison camp, he relaxed, "goldbricking" in the vernacular of the day, speaking fluent German with the inmates. This, after all, was someone with twenty foreign languages in his linguistic repertoire. Three years earlier, Harvard had awarded him a degree in comparative philology—the study of languages—magna cum laude, Phi Beta Kappa. Undoubtedly, he played chess and cards and imbibed in barracks-made alcoholic concoctions, talking about Germany, its government and the war but primarily using the time to scout out perspective sojourners for his upcoming journey, one destined to lead much farther than a prisoner of war stockade a hundred yards away and intended to be for life, not a weekend. Everything known about this tridurnal visit came out a few weeks later during an investigation of another matter—that is, on more or less a fluke. One wonders how often this private skulked back and forth between the U.S. Army base and the prisoner of war camp or how often he would have continued these forbidden sorties in the weeks and months ahead had he chosen to fulfill his Germanomania through frequent short trips here and there rather than playing an all-or-nothing hand, one grand sweep to shoot the moon.

At about 4:30 p.m. on a February afternoon in 1944, just south of Old Palomas, Chihuahua, Mexico, a Mexican customs official named Medordo Martínez Mejía apprehended three migrants as they furtively meandered a couple hundred yards from the road before starting to hitchhike.

Maybe these were prisoners of war from a camp in Texas or New Mexico. This being wartime, reports of escaping prisoners were not uncommon, and it was not at all unusual they would head to Mexico, notorious for its network of German agents who operated a well-coordinated underground railroad transporting prisoners, saboteurs and spies. Make it to Mexico and a prisoner could be on his way to Brazil, Argentina, Germany—nearly anywhere.

Mejía detained the vagabonds by the side of the road until a horse-drawn wagon came along, which he used to transport them to the Mexican Customs House, where he turned them over to his boss, José Magnana Zaragoza. A U.S. immigration inspector named William Bates, stationed in Columbus, New Mexico, was called and immediately drove the three miles from the U.S. Customs House to the Mexican Customs House, about one hundred yards south of the border, to fetch the Gang of Three.

The nomadic trio's putative leader said his name was Eduard Müeller and that he was a German soldier who had escaped from a prisoner of war camp. He provided his prisoner identity card, signed his name with the umlaut, answered questions in a thick German accent and showed difficulty with speaking English. He talked about his family, life and schooling back in Germany and his duties as a German soldier. He carried a little bag containing a change of underwear, a cured ham and an electric razor. The two pauciloquent sojourners traveling with him carried typical escapee travel items, such as candy bars, pocketknives and compasses, but they also had a few unusual items, including little flags and a personal letter touting Germany's strengths. The letter was in German, so it couldn't be translated until later. But there was no mistaking the swastikas on the flags.

Doña Ana Courthouse. *Courtesy of the Doña Ana Sheriff's Department.*

Inspector Bates believed the two silent men were not the Jewish refugees from Europe looking for work as they originally claimed but, rather, were the prisoners of war who had just been reported missing a few days earlier from a camp in Amarillo, Texas. Bates turned them over to the FBI to figure it out.

At about noon the next day, February 19, 1944, at the Doña Ana County Jail in Las Cruces, New Mexico, a legendary lawman nicknamed "Jellybean" interviewed the disheveled itinerant named Müeller. Here fame collided with infamy, renown with notoriety; the man on one side of the desk would later have books written about him and be featured in *Life Magazine*, the other in *Time*.

# 1
# Harvard Graduate to Army Private

Dale H. Maple, class of 1941, was mentioned twice in the November 14, 1940 issue of the *Crimson*. The Harvard newspaper mentioned in one article that he was 1 of 114 students awarded scholarships for marked excellence. In another, it reported he had been summarily dismissed from Harvard's Reserve Officers Training Corps (ROTC) because of his Nazi sympathies.

Maple entered Harvard in 1937, a few days before his seventeenth birthday. Before 1940, the *Crimson* had mentioned Maple a couple times, including once in his freshman year, reporting he had been dealt a perfect hand of thirteen hearts in a bridge game, with the odds calculated for the reader at fifty million to one. The *Boston American* also reported this extraordinary rarity and included in its story a photo of Maple. Later, it was revealed the bridge hand was perpetrated by a prankster stacking the cards. It wasn't mentioned whether Maple was in on the fraud. Maple and his friends, according to a classmate who later became Maple's lawyer, were notorious for pulling off astonishing hoaxes.[1]

Maple had said several times that his most enjoyable experiences during his undergraduate years were as a member of the Glee Club but his notoriety related to his ROTC membership. On campus, he sometimes wore bold clothes that didn't match, according to a classmate, but usually he wore his ROTC uniform, even on non-drill days. Maple stated in the Harvard yearbook that his home town was Middletown, Rhode Island, and that teaching was his intended vocation. With the exception of the years from 1937 to 1950, he lived in and around San Diego all his life.[2]

Since the age of fourteen, Maple had participated in ROTC, dreaming of becoming a soldier. He joined his junior high school's ROTC and followed it through to San Diego High School, where he graduated first in his class of 585 students. At least 1 of his high school teachers suspected trouble ahead for Maple for several reasons, including his preferences for authoritarian governments, predicting Maple would end up a fascist.[3] Maple, the outlandish maverick, enjoyed agitating, even in high school, consistently staking out contrarian and shocking positions. But there's no record of whether this rebel kept a bust of Hitler back then in San Diego, which is something he did later in his college dorm room.

The ROTC expulsions should not have come as a surprise to anyone. Maple had just made national news a couple weeks earlier when *Time* magazine published "Making of a Nazi," identifying him as perhaps the most notorious college student in America:

> *Dale H. Maple, 20, is a clean-cut U.S. boy, with hazel eyes, white, even teeth, a firm, straight jaw. Born in San Diego, Calif. to middle-class U.S. parents, he went to San Diego High school, shone in his studies, showed talent in music. A devout Catholic, he attended church every Sunday. In school he studied German, became interested in German culture. He graduated from high school age 16. At home, affairs went less well. His father and mother eventually separated. His father wanted Dale to be a chemical engineer, his mother, a diplomat. Three years ago Dale entered Harvard. To please his mother, he concentrated on history the first year; second year, to please his father he majored in chemistry. Third year, he pleased himself, concentrated on comparative philology—because he had always wanted to be a linguist. Shy and unhappy, Dale made few friends, immersed himself in the study of difficult languages—Assyrian, Catalan, Hungarian. For relaxation, he joined the Verein Turmwachter (Harvard's German Club), became its treasurer. With fellow club members, he spoke German, drank beer, sang German songs, heard German speakers, discussed German culture. For all their Germanic carousing, his companions remained good democrats. But they soon began to discern in Dale Maple a growing admiration for Adolf Hitler, and for Nazi "efficiency." Dale took perverse pleasure in shocking his associates by singing the Horst Wessel song and Deutschland Uber Alles. When pink-cheeked Faculty Advisor James Hawkes became perturbed and tried to squelch his Nazi talk, Dale conceived a cordial dislike for Instructor Hawkes, became still more defiant. To the dismay of his roommate, Dale installed a bust of Hitler on his desk. Last week Dale Maple shocked arch-*

> *patriotic Harvard by resigning from the Verein Turmwachter and publicly applauding Hitler and all his works. To the Harvard* Crimson*'s editors, who could scarcely believe their ears, he defiantly exclaimed: "Even a bad dictatorship is better than a good democracy." To educators, Dale Maple's case proved little about Harvard, much about the psychology of frustration.*[4]

Incidentally, as an ironic glimpse of what loomed ahead, an advertisement touting security fences appeared on the same page as this article in *Time*. It was captioned: *It Takes More Than a Sign to Keep Out Saboteurs*.

Shortly before his banishment from ROTC, Maple voluntarily resigned from Harvard's German Club. His resignation letter, replete with pro-German sentiments, garnered for Maple a bit of notoriety. The *Crimson* noted, among other things, that Maple preferred to live under a totalitarian regime and had justified Hitler's atrocities under the pretext of necessity. The newspapers reported little at the time about either the resignation or the dismissal, according to a later *New Yorker* story, because they were investigating other stories. When Maple resigned from the German Club, the papers were focusing on Dr. Herbert Scholtz, the German Counsel in Boston, because a local politician at that time was demanding an investigation of Dr. Scholtz. Not surprisingly, Maple had been in communication with Dr. Scholtz, but apparently no one pursued the connection at the time. No one knew then that Maple was working with Dr. Scholtz to obtain passage to Berlin, ostensibly to work for a news agency. A few years later, *New Yorker* writer and Harvard graduate Ely Jacques Kahn, better known as E. J. Kahn, observed that the Sunday *New York Times* had buried a simple notice about Maple's dismissal on page 28, in the middle of column five. Kahn later noted that in October 1940, the

Maple finished first in his high school class of 585 students. *Courtesy of the San Diego High School Alumni Association.*

*Boston Globe* reported the Boston office of Dr. Scholtz and the San Francisco German Counselor Office were hotbeds of Nazi propaganda.[5]

When the ROTC dismissal story hit, the papers were glued to news of the Dies Congressional Committee, which had just announced plans to investigate not only Dr. Scholtz but also all German and Italian counselors living in the United States. Again, Maple temporarily stayed under the media radar.

Meanwhile, while all this was going on at Harvard, the U.S. Congress was actively looking into the matter of Nazi sympathizers, and Communists too. In 1938, the U.S. House of Representatives had formed a committee to investigate "the extent, character, and objects of un-American propaganda activities in the United States." Although originally limited to eight months, the committee, headed by Representative Martin Dies Jr., continued for years. In 1945, it was renamed the House Committee on Un-American Activities. The committee stated that Congress did not have the power to deny citizens the right to believe in Communism, Fascism or Nazism, but it did have the right to bring attention to their activities. The controversial committee focused on identifying Nazis and Communists in America, asserting 6 million of them were out there posing a national security threat. The committee provided to the attorney general a list of some 1,100 federal employees whom it identified as members of subversive organizations. The FBI and the attorney general dismissed the allegations as grandstanding bunk; the secretary of the interior characterized Congressman Dies as the "outstanding zany of American political history."[6]

Dale Maple later claimed that in 1940, he was not a Nazi and didn't really understand what the term meant; instead he was simply trying to garner a fervent pro-German reputation. Such publicity, he believed, would get the attention of the German government and, in the process, provide him an opportunity to pursue a doctorate degree at the University of Berlin. He spoke of his zealous Nazism in stolid, casual terms. This puzzling insouciance led one doctor to later opine: "He appears to have absorbed all the Nazi philosophies without being aware of their enormity or significance. As if [he] carried a bracelet of poisonous rattlers without realizing the degree of harm that he might thus spread."[7]

Maple's high school teachers and principal, normally sorry to see honor students graduate, were greatly relieved when Maple graduated. He often asked teachers difficult questions in class that they either couldn't answer or, if they could, trapped them in unwinnable debates with the brilliant student. Sometimes Maple answered the questions himself, and often he returned to school after class to finish the discussion. "It might be on science, philosophy, higher math, or world affairs, and we [would] all breathe easier in our classrooms," one administrator said, "not wondering as he sat there apparently dreaming, what question he was going to ask of a most complex nature." Maple, the principal opined, didn't need college at all. With just books, a little time and "that imagination of his, he will absorb all there is in any book and then produce his own theory on the subject."[8] An army report stated: "He graduated from high school at the top of his class, the faculty breathing sighs of relief because of the difficulties they had experienced in keeping pace with [Maple's] intellectual development and their own embarrassment at their frequent inability to answer his pertinent and searching questions."[9]

Had it been somehow possible to combine all high school seniors in America in 1937 into one single class, Maple would have finished at or near the very top. His high school ROTC thesis explained the trajectory of a bullet. A psychologist pegged his IQ at 152 but believed it was actually higher.[10] He spoke or had a solid comprehension of at least twenty foreign languages, including Russian, Polish, German, Hungarian, Italian, Spanish, Portuguese, Danish, Swedish, Icelandic, Dutch, French, Latin, Greek, Sanskrit, Babylonian, Assyrian, Hebrew, Arabic and Maltese.

Maple's father later claimed in 1944 that his son, who was twenty-three at the time, was "just a boy with all the fanciful dreams and ideals and imaginations of a boy. A man with the mind of almost a genius, a mind that grasps the knowledge of the deepest science almost with the reading of the printed word, a brain capable of absorbing knowledge at a rate almost unbelievable." Maple worked, his father said, "in the extreme, never half-way or with moderation, always plung[ing] into the most difficult task and emerg[ing] with top honors."[11] As a student of history, according to a friend, Maple could rattle off details of any major or minor battle from the last 2,500 years. He mastered the theory of calculus by himself in a few days, learned Gregg short hand in six weeks and taught himself how to play the pipe organ. He was so skilled at the pipe organ and piano that he performed works of Bach, Chopin, Beethoven and Liszt in numerous recitals, including as a soloist in November 1935 at the California Pacific International Exposition, otherwise known as the San Diego World's Fair. A newspaper reviewer praised one of Maple's early musical performances: "The exhibition's program material bespoke a commendable desire on the part of the young student to reach the best in piano literature in his first appearance before the public. Memorizing the long and difficult program was no small achievement in itself."[12]

POW Camp Douglas, Wyoming. *Courtesy of the Gates Frontier Fund Wyoming within the Carol M. Highsmith Archive, Library of Congress, Prints and Photographs Collection.*

The other students in music class, according to the instructor, didn't particularly care for Maple because of his superior intellect and musical proficiency. His hands were slightly webbed, requiring an operation if he wished to become a concert artist, which he could have become, his music teacher noted. But Harvard and academics interested him more than music.[13]

The San Diego World's Fair featured some controversial and unusual exhibits, such as a silver robot named "Alpha," an old Globe Shakespearean Theatre, a midget city on a doll-house scale (with more than one hundred midgets) and "Zoro Gardens," a nudist colony led by Zorine, Queen of the Nudists. For twenty-five cents, spectators ogled nudists as they played volleyball and generally lounged around. Those unwilling or unable to pay peeped through openings in the fence. The fair attracted nearly seven million visitors, about twice as many as had attended the world's fair twenty years earlier—not bad for the middle of an economic depression.[14]

Maple's father, L.G. Maple, and mother, Mae Cleo Harris, were originally from Mapleton, Illinois (outside Peoria), and Kuttawa, Kentucky, respectively, and married on July 20, 1915, in San Bernardino, California, in a ceremony, according to the wedding blurb, beneath the cross on top of Mount Rubidoux.[15] They divorced in about 1938. After the divorce, she moved east, to Newport, Rhode Island, and married Edwin Scoville. L.G. Maple stayed in San Diego and also remarried. According to an obituary in the *San Diego Union-Tribune*, one day in about 1940, L.G. Maple came across a woman distraught over missing the bus to take her from her Ocean Beach home to the downtown San Diego restaurant where she worked. He offered the stranded woman a ride in his car, consoled her and ended up marrying her. Together they bought a four-acre plot in the San Diego suburb of Encanto where they grew avocadoes. Maple had no siblings. It appears he never married or had children.[16]

During summer breaks at Harvard, Maple worked in San Diego for his father in the wholesale aluminum and steel business, as a boilermaker in a dredging company, as a chauffeur, prospecting for gold in Nevada and in an ROTC camp. He graduated from Harvard in the spring of 1941, with a senior thesis titled "A Statistical Investigation of Early Germanic Dialects, with Special Reference to Problems in the Classification of Dialects and Languages."

## Maple Joins the Army

After graduation, Maple was offered a job in the defense industry in California at Consolidated Aircraft, but the offer was quickly rescinded with no explanation before he started work. It was likely that his notoriety marked him as a security risk. He returned to Harvard to study for a master's degree in languages and obtained employment in the university's physics department working on radios and microphones. Again, he was promptly discharged for security reasons. He suspected both job terminations resulted from information provided by the FBI.

In a letter to *New Yorker* writer E.J. Kahn, FBI director John Edgar Hoover noted, however, that he couldn't say whether FBI information caused the terminations. Hoover didn't explain whether he couldn't say because he didn't know or because he didn't think it advisable to share the information. Hoover replied to Kahn's questions that yes, indeed, one of Maple's friends from Harvard had been extremely pro-Nazi and had probably influenced Maple's ideas about the Third Reich. Hoover stated the FBI had terminated its inquiry of this student and turned its files over to military authorities once the FBI learned the former student was in the U.S. Army.[17]

At about this time, Pearl Harbor got bombed, bringing the United States into the war. Maple called Dr. Scholtz on December 8, 1941, to inquire about getting to Germany with the diplomatic staff. In a very short conversation, Dr. Scholtz said it was too late.

Realizing he had been fired from two jobs because of his suspected Nazi sympathies, Maple believed the only way he could "prove" his patriotism to America was to join the U.S. military and become a loyal soldier, so on February 27, 1942, in Boston, he enlisted in the U.S. Army for the duration of the war plus six months. He had not been drafted. The navy had first rejected him, not for his reputation or political views but because of ear problems. He withdrew from Harvard on March 10, 1942.

He was first sent to Fort Bragg, North Carolina, and assigned to the Field Artillery Replacement Training Center. Life in the army wasn't bad. Maple wrote often to his mother, asking in one letter that she ship his piano to him. He enjoyed the power of responsibility, noting, "I had the pleasure of putting under arrest this morning one boy just returning from a 17-day vacation without leave." One day in June 1942, Maple boasted that he was in complete charge "of everybody and everything."[18]

He applied for glider and parachute training but became so frustrated with delays that after months of waiting, he requested a transfer to the Seventy-Sixth Division, a small combat unit at Fort Meade, Maryland. There he became a radio operator and instructor and was assigned to a task force of replacements in the Africa Campaign. He applied to Officer's Candidate School, but according to Maple, the application languished and orders to ship out to Africa were canceled. He never got army life insurance, so perhaps he never got close to shipping out.

Military intelligence knew of Maple's pro-Hitler sentiments. As part of a strategy to segregate into dedicated companies those soldiers suspected of disloyalty to the United States, the army set up so-called special organizations, including the 620th Engineer General Service Company in Fort Meade, South Dakota, with the first soldiers reporting in November 1942. Previously, these soldiers had been integrated into army ranks, where they could fly under the radar and go relatively unnoticed. The U.S. military had to decide whether to keep soldiers suspected of disloyalty in the military or discharge them. Either approach carried risks. Keeping the soldiers in uniform could lead to sabotage, but the upside was the military could observe them.

On March 22, 1943, Maple was promoted to private first class and assigned to the 1367th Service Unit at Indiantown Gap, Pennsylvania, a temporary holding place while the army determined the soldiers' loyalty and decided to which special organization the disloyal soldiers would be assigned. The army got behind on these loyalty investigations, so it took a while to segregate the

Italian prisoners at the Fort Knox Canteen. *Courtesy of General George Patton Museum and Center of Leadership.*

soldiers into separate camps. Until the army determined and instituted a consistent policy, the soldiers suspected of disloyalty trained like other soldiers in every aspect. Commanders dealt with this sensitive issue on an ad-hoc basis. Two weeks after his assignment to the 1367th, Maple was transferred to the 620th EGS in Fort Meade. "It's something very extraordinary and it is not a shipment overseas," Maple wrote. "The transfer has all the battalion in an uproar since no one knows what it's all about."[19]

## Special Organizations

The 620th, consisting of just one company of about two hundred men, was one of the army's special organizations, units featuring a mix of nationalities and political beliefs, mostly Germans and Italians, cross-pollinated with Finns, Russians, Hungarians, Communists, a Yugoslavian and a few others. The 1943 Thanksgiving menu listed two officers, fifty-eight noncommissioned officers, forty-nine privates first class and eighty-six privates. Some of the soldiers earned their placement in these organizations by saying or doing things demonstrably disloyal to the United States; others were there because they were born in Germany. Some were bitter enemies of America who vowed to assist the enemy; others stated they would fight for the United States but not against their home countries.

Altogether approximately 1,200 to 1,500 American soldiers were assigned to these special organizations: the 620th at Fort Meade, the 358th Quartermaster Service Company and the 525th Quartermaster Service Company. The 358th was originally established in August 1942 at Virginia's Camp A.P. Hill. A month later, it was transferred to Camp Riley, near Little Falls, Minnesota, and in April 1943, it moved to Camp Carson, Colorado. The 525th was organized at Fort Leonard Wood, Missouri, in July 1943. After the war, the special organizations were merged together.

Not issued weapons, these soldiers immediately realized upon arrival that their units were "thinly disguised as military organizations."[20] One soldier observed that everyone spoke with an accent and no one in ordinary army ranks trusted them. These weren't regular army units. Outsiders often referred to the camps as "snake pits" or "snake farms."[21] With make-work assignments like garnishing camouflage nets, pulling weeds, sawing wood, transplanting trees, maintaining roads and cleaning up the post, the members took umbrage in their new assignments and often carped that noncommissioned officers took particular delight in giving them menial, degrading tasks.

Waxing patriotic about how they had voluntarily joined the army to show their loyalty and to fight for America, many noted they had successfully and proudly begun their military careers with no problems. Suddenly, and without explanation—or, at least, no explanation given—they ended up in the 620th, an embarrassing situation to them and to family members at home who eventually got wind that the 620th consisted of soldiers considered subversive.

Members of the special organizations usually communicated with other special organizations through family members. Notes, gifts and cigarettes got exchanged, especially on holidays. On at least two occasions in early 1944, members of the 620th traveled to Denver to socialize and exchange information with members of the 358th at Camp Carson. According to army reports, swastikas were displayed in a hotel room that had been reserved under a fictitious name.

Despite the soldiers' complaints, the 620th enjoyed the time and freedom at Fort Meade to come and go as they pleased. Shortly after arriving in

POWs were held in 660 camps throughout the United States. *Courtesy of the Mississippi Armed Forces Museum–Birdsong Collection.*

the spring of 1943, a few of them—the "inner group," aka the "executive committee," "group of nine" or "high command"—rented a house for forty dollars per month in Spearfish Canyon. The house, known as the Rim Rock Lodge, served as a weekend cabin by invitation only to trustworthy members. For five dollars per weekend, the retreat offered an ideal secluded setting to relax, hike, fish and drink. For fifty cents, Private Frederich Siering ferried men in his Oldsmobile convertible back and forth between Fort Meade and the lodge. Maple estimated about forty men of the 620th visited the lodge at some point during the summer of 1943. In addition, the inner group members also met occasionally by themselves in the basement of a house on Main Street in nearby Sturgis, South Dakota.

Consisting of ten barracks of twenty men each, the Fort Meade base boasted a faux German village set up for close-quarter combat training. The soldiers loved getting their pictures taken there, in front of the biergarten signs. With minimal restrictions, they could pretty much come and go as they wanted. They could stay out at the nearby Deadwood all-night bars without having to get a pass. Several rented apartments in Deadwood. Maple shared an apartment for twenty-nine dollars a month, plus utilities, with Theophil Leonhard and Paul Kissman, two men who play prominently in this story. If the soldiers couldn't find a friend to drive them to Deadwood, they could take a bus.

The true disloyalists and the suspected disloyalists of the 620th whipped up myriad schemes in their spare time, including some involving espionage and sabotage. Of the special organizations, the 620th was the most likely to do something drastic, but its members differed over how to best vent their enmity. One recurring theme that everyone agreed on, however, dealt with ferreting out and punishing "stool pigeons," those "polishing the apple"—that is, currying favor with authorities by snitching on fellow comrades.

The peace faction of the 620th eschewed violence, arguing publicity alone would be the panacea to set them free. The American public, they believed, would demand the camps be shut down, but only if the media could be cajoled to explain the plight of these American soldiers, some with no blemishes on their military records: they were segregated into camps, relegated to the sidelines and made extraneous rather than useful in the critical war effort. They would try to contact influential Americans, including widely read columnists. Private Arthur Luck claimed he knew people who could get in contact with prominent Americans like Charles Lindbergh, Henry Ford and Father Coughlin.

The militant faction of the 620th favored revolt—a putsch in the Dakota Black Hills, seizing arms and using force, preferably in coordination with other special organizations—to wage guerrilla warfare throughout the United States, with a mutiny scheduled for late spring 1944. Maple said he knew a soldier stationed at Camp Carson who might participate, but information indicated Camp Carson soldiers were reluctant to get involved because two of their men had been sent to prison for fraternizing with prisoners of war.

The army knew of these sinister meetings and also knew about the large cache of dynamite, caps and fuses found about a half mile south of Rim Rock Lodge, near where group members hiked. But since the explosives couldn't be tied to members of the 620th, not much happened other than a few reports being written. A lieutenant colonel reported that the 620th was a group of subversives, extremely bitter about being in the unit. He opined that most members had at least a general knowledge of the violence planned by its militant members.

When members of the 620th were later confronted about their plans of violence, the plotters dismissed their discussions as the innocuous chatter of provocateurs, not conspiring saboteurs—palaver, not perfidy. And if they had been serious, they claimed, the actions would occur only as a defensive strategy to be activated in a national emergency, such as if the United States was taken over by Communists, and only until law and order could be restored. There were no known acts of sabotage while the 620th was at Fort Meade, and the worst trouble Dale Maple got into related to tampering with someone's car, a puzzling, unexplained charge.

In one army report, an investigator rated the likelihood of each soldier escaping or engaging in sabotage. Most members of the 620th generally fell in the "unknown" category, but a few were written off as too psychologically weak or too stupid. One, for example, was characterized as "not too intelligent" and thus wouldn't be a likely prospect for inclusion in either an escape or a mutiny. Others were "not mentally equipped to be of any particular danger" or didn't appear to be "sufficient[ly] aggressiveness to participate in anything of this nature."

The army had general knowledge of the schemes at the time, but most of the details didn't come out until later. The army didn't know, for example, that members of the inner group had a map at the lodge showing the Mexican coast, detailed with depths and currents, or that the group kept a roster of the 620th with approximately forty names checked off—those considered trustworthy for sabotage planning. The army didn't learn until later about these discussions, much of it generated by the most vocal and indiscreet member of the 620th: Eric Bell Hotelling, whom Maple called a "walking encyclopedia."[22] Hotelling stood out from the rest, assiduously pushing "grandiosely intellectual and preposterous" ideas at every opportunity, filtering his communications through what an army intelligence report characterized as a modified Julius Caesar cipher system.[23] Hotelling's plans, and there's no reason to believe Maple and the others were not on board, featured the men of the 620th taking over the camp and, working with the other special organizations, fomenting mayhem and destruction throughout the United States, starting with destroying bridges and cutting phone lines. All this would be made possible through a "shuttle system" transporting an army of saboteurs back and forth between Germany and America. Not surprisingly, Hotelling appointed himself in charge, with the rank of brigadier general.

Maple attended some of the meetings but was generally viewed as a lone wolf with a minimal role in social activities. But he certainly didn't have to be inveigled into duplicity. There's evidence he was one of the masterminds and that he intentionally kept a low profile. He certainly knew the benefit of doing so. After all, his comments and actions landed him in *Time* in October 1940. Maple later was asked whether he was a member of the "high command" of the 620th. He said he wasn't exactly a member but he was associated with it. Hotelling later wrote that he had it on "unimpeachable authority" that Maple planned as early as September 1943 to escape and take up life in South America under a new identity.[24]

By the end of 1943, the army had become concerned enough to act. On December 5, the 620th was transferred from Fort Meade to Camp Hale, Colorado. The snow and altitude of the Rockies and the presence of Nazi prisoners of war created an obstacle or, at least, a perceived hindrance to any ruminations of potential mutineers. Perhaps the thinking was that the army guards already at Camp Hale watching hundreds of prisoners of war could also keep watch on members of the 620th at the same time. There had

Cold-weather warfare training at Camp Hale in the Rockies. *Courtesy of the Tenth Mountain Division Resource Center, Denver Public Library.*

been no prisoners of war at Fort Meade with the 620th.[25] Enclosed within a wooden fence topped with barbed wire, the Camp Hale prisoner of war camp was a side camp for Denver's Camp Trinidad. The distance from the 620th camp to the prison barracks ranged in estimates from 60 to 150 yards.

Camp Hale served as a training ground for winter and mountain warfare. Those pictures of troops skiing represented work, not play. Join the army and go skiing it could have said. The military installation at Camp Hale served as home to the Tenth Mountain Division, the Thirty-Eighth Regimental Combat Team and the Ninety-Ninth Infantry Battalion.

## Tension Heats Up in the Mountains

Two factors at Camp Hale created heightened rancor among the soldiers of the 620th. First, the army denied some privileges the soldiers had previously enjoyed at Fort Meade and thus had come to expect, such as married soldiers living off base and all soldiers being allowed to own and drive personal automobiles. In January 1944, members of the 620th were told, with no explanation given, to sell their personal cars or put them into storage. Maple, according to a fellow soldier, said he felt like going out and buying a car just to test this restriction. The soldiers also complained about their mail being reviewed without a censor's stamp and of being monitored constantly, even while on furlough.

Another factor escalating ire in "Camp Hell," as the soldiers often called it,[26] related to the army's suddenly enforcing the prohibition against fraternizing with prisoners. Upon arriving at Camp Hale, members of the 620th enjoyed talking with the prisoners, sharing stories about family, friends and places back in Germany, and asking about brothers and cousins serving in the German army or navy. After all, these American soldiers were in the 620th because they were alleged or real Germanophiles. In fact, some were actually German citizens.[27]

## Cracking Down

At first, the army didn't enforce the rules about fraternizing with prisoners. But it didn't take long to crack down. Placing the 620th next to the prisoner of war stockade and then prohibiting communication between the groups escalated tension. The early and brief opportunity to communicate had quickly become the standard. To the men of the 620th, taking it away seemed arbitrary and punitive.

Later, several members told investigators that it was immediately clear to them there might be problems. One soldier warned that placing the prisoners and the 620th next to each other was like giving matches to a kid. Various members suspected "serious trouble would be the consequence" and feared "trouble would ultimately develop."[28] Another said:

> *The climax was reached upon our transfer to Camp Hale. Without possibly realizing the psychological effect, we were assigned to barracks within a comparatively few yards of the German Prisoner of War stockade, and almost the next day our details brought us into close proximity, as they were doing work quite close to most of our details. Needless to say many of our men became familiar with them. I did not talk to them. The singing of the prisoners as they marched had a psychological effect.... To some the effect was hypnotic, the hypnosis seeming to have a lasting effect.... The impending crisis was*

*outwardly noticeable.... The temptations were seemingly placed in our way on purpose and many were too weak to resist them.*[29]

"It appears," one report noted, "that the sight of these prisoners had a profound effect on [members of the 620th], particularly those of German birth. Members of this company began talking with the German prisoners of war, exchanging notes with them, and giving them small gifts."[30]

Subsequent army reports stated in various words that it wasn't advisable to place a camp of pro-German American soldiers suspected or proven to be disloyal next to a prisoner of war camp holding hundreds of captured German soldiers. Certainly, by this point, Maple's Nazi sympathies were widely known.[31]

Maple talked openly about challenging the restriction against talking with prisoners, hinting at the sensation it would cause if something big occurred between army soldiers and prisoners. Perhaps at that point, Maple opined, the War Department would realize the folly of placing the 620th next door

Also stationed at Camp Hale were the 620th Engineers—U.S. Army soldiers suspected of disloyalty. *Courtesy of David Witte.*

to prisoners of war and then not expecting the two groups to communicate. Private Maple occasionally saw some of the prisoners and got to know them fairly well. Like most of the members of the 620th, he occasionally gave the prisoners cigarettes and candy bars.

Another source of bitterness resulted from the change of camp commander, which happened about the same time as the transfer from Fort Meade to Camp Hale. In the transfer, members of the 620th lost Louis Hutton, a deferential officer; in his place, they picked up the restrictive Leroy Wilson, who struck members of the 620th as a mean-spirited oppressor who relished the opportunity to make life as unpleasant for them as long and as often as he could. By late January 1944, with the arbitrary removal of the cars, the secret review of the mail, the change to a harsh commander and the perceived punitive restriction of communicating with the prisoners, the enmity of the 620th, which had started back at Fort Meade, rose to a boiling point. The soldiers and prisoners still exchanged cigarettes, gifts and messages, but did so covertly now. In the process, the "cabal flouted and defied the officers at every opportunity."[32]

The sabotage plans that had been discussed back at Fort Meade were resurrected, this time with added gusto and unique possibilities thanks to the presence of hundreds of Nazi soldiers itching to escape, penned up just a hundred yards away. Another lagniappe dropped into the intrigue were the women stationed in the WAC (Women's Army Corps) barracks next door, directly between Camp Hale and the prisoner of war stockade. Several WACs would prove helpful in the clandestine communications between the 620th and the prisoners.

## Warped Personality

Maple's actions were blamed on various factors, including a childhood accident, a warped personality, a hypnotic trance and simply being too smart for his own good. His former pastor at the Baptist church stated that on Easter Sunday 1929, a speeding motorist hit Maple as the congregation dispensed from church. The young lad was carried into the church and laid on the speaker's platform, "where he flopped about like a dying chicken," causing the pastor and others to wonder if this concussed youth might do bizarre and unpredictable things later in life. The pastor, Orson Jones, claimed there wasn't any formal written record of the accident on file, because the police weren't contacted at that time since the driver, a high school boy, felt so broken-hearted and penitent.[33]

Maple's father claimed the accident left Dale in a daze and severely "scattered the brain jelly" so much that he worried it might cause unaccountable quirks later in life. He said his son's mind was unbalanced and his judgment not developed. Dale's parents worried during Maple's grade school years that teachers moved him along too quickly for his own emotional and psychological good and that he would be out in the world before he had time to grow up.[34] To keep Maple busy, the school regularly gave him a pass to help out in the office and do anything he wanted. In 1950, Tom Pickett, a member of the House of Representatives, weighed in at the behest of a constituent who was trying to obtain the records from the army but was having difficulty because the files were still labeled as secret: "[Dale Maple's] father and mother were divorced. It is my understanding this resulted in the boy having a warped personality. The published reports state that a sanity commission was appointed and [found] him sane although the affect of the divided home had a bearing on his mental attitude."[35]

A fellow soldier blamed Maple's "extremely rash act which could not have been attempted in a rational state of mind" on Maple's hypnotized state, caused by the singing of German soldiers as they marched by the 620th camp.[36] A professor at the New York State College of Home Economics at Cornell University named Russell C. Smart contacted the army in October 1947 saying he wanted to use Dale Maple as a case study in his class. Professor Smart was an expert in the field of child development and relationships, having authored and coauthored several books on the subject. Smart, in fact, did later use Dale Maple as a subject in a book, and he included in that book a reprint of the October 1940 *Time* article, followed by a practical exercise to "discuss the items in Dale Maple's history which made him behave the way he did."[37] On the theme of personality, several years later, in 1959, the State of California published a report titled *The Emotionally Handicapped Child and the School: A Research Program in the Prevention of Personality and Behavior Disorders in Children.* Emotionally handicapped children, the report warned, "may appear mentally retarded or extremely brilliant," which then led into a short biography of Dale Maple.[38]

Maple's Harvard tutor purportedly warned that "no one brain could stand what Dale was trying to cram into it."[39] The tutor was anxiously waiting to see what the results would be a few years later. One military psychiatrist concluded Maple's actions were "definitely not of psychotic proportions." The problem, the doctor noted, was society and the schools. It was

> *a pathetic indictment of the parental and educational influences to which he was exposed that this "intellectual genius" could proceed through life and graduate from a university without absorbing any emotional warmth or developing any lasting attachments and criteria of adult behavior beyond the philosophical rationalizations which singled him out for outbursts of publicity and notoriety.*[40]

Harvard, class of 1941. *Courtesy of HUD 341.04, Harvard University Archives.*

A Harvard classmate named Charles O. Porter, who became Maple's attorney, pointed out Maple's history of conducting "astonishing hoaxes," the inference being an innocent desire to shock was Maple's motivation. "I think it is plain," Porter opined, "that he [had] tremendously bad judgment due to the effect of genius in warping his balanced growth to maturity."[41]

## He Looked Fishy at Harvard

By the spring of 1944, far removed from her former San Diego life and home, a forty-seven-year-old woman newly relocated in Rhode Island had started her new life in Newport, volunteering with social, religious and women's groups; raising money for worthwhile causes; and getting mentioned in the society pages. Here she's a committee member of the Aquidneck Chapter, Order of the Eastern Star; a month later she's the hospitality coordinator for the Newport Business and Professional Women's Club. Then she's organizing the annual Christmas party and plays a prominent role as a team captain for an event sponsored by the Newport Community Chest. But Mae Cleo Scoville (née Harris, formerly Maple) would have traded all the newspaper clippings to do away with this one, a mother's worst dream and a society woman's nightmare, a whisper-inducing headline in the *Newport Mercury and Weekly News*: "Newporter's Kin Charged with Treason."

Imagine seeing that in your local newspaper and, furthermore, in a small town back when newspapers often listed home addresses in the articles. Indeed, subsequent newspaper articles reported her address and the fact that she was married to Edwin Scoville, a sheet metal worker at the Naval Torpedo Station. It was big news in Newport, as well as around the world, and it set off a diplomatic imbroglio in the U.S. government. Officials from the State Department as well as the Immigration and Naturalization Service got involved, the United States and the Mexican Customs Services played roles, and the Department of War argued with the Department of Justice over who would prosecute Maple. The FBI wanted to know the details, the army needed to know who else was involved in the escape and Howard Houk, the U.S. District Attorney for New Mexico, wanted to determine the source of the funds used to finance the escape, a topic causing Mae no little angst since she had just given her son \$150.[42] At the same time, Maple obtained \$200 from his father, ostensibly for college expenses but actually to build a getaway pelf, starting with \$250 for a 1934 Reo "Flying Cloud" automobile.

Others chipping in to help finance Maple with cash and gas ration coupons included some soldiers of the 620$^{th}$, as well as prisoners of war. Private First Class Dale Maple, who earned \$54.00 per month from the army, less \$18.75 for government savings bonds, landed in *Time* once again:

> *Nazi Bent*
>
> *Dale Maple is a tall quick-witted young man with a ruddy face and ready grin. Covered with scholastic honors from San Diego High School at 16, he later went to Harvard. There he was bounced out of a German Club for singing Nazi hymns, out of the R.O.T.C. for Nazi sympathies. The FBI looked him over, turned a fishy eye on him, but all was forgiven when Harvard-man Maple enlisted in the Army. Private Maple was finally detailed to Colorado's Camp Hale, where some German prisoners of war were confined. As might have been expected, Maple struck up a friendship with two of the superrace. One Tuesday morning he reported for sick leave. Several days later, south of the Mexican border, immigration officials picked up three men in U.S. Army uniforms. One of them turned out to be Maple. The others were*

> *his Nazi friends, who were on their way by some "underground," they hoped, to Germany. Maple, according to FBI officials, was on his way with them; he preferred the German Government. Round-faced Sergeant Heinrich Kikillus, 32, and hard-faced Sergeant Erhard Schwichtenberg, sometime members of Rommel's hard-boiled* Afrika Korps, *were held as witnesses. Their punishment will not be hard. Private Maple, of the U.S. Army, was held for a court-martial. The crime with which he is charged: treason, for which the top punishment is death.*[43]

The photo of Maple, taken shortly after his apprehension, was captioned: "He looked fishy at Harvard." Maple's mother first heard about it from an Associated Press reporter who called her at home asking for a comment. Thus, she had advance notice before the story was printed to alert some friends. The article reported she was shocked to hear the news. She didn't believe any of it and had no idea how her son could get involved in such a thing. She had just received a letter from her son on February 14, saying one of his friends at Camp Hale was in trouble and was to be court-martialed. Dale claimed he was the only one who could help the friend and he was working day and night to do so. (The case Maple referred to concerned Fritz Loock.) Maple remarked in his letter to his mother that it might be a long time before she heard from him again.

Remnants of Camp Greeley, Colorado. *Courtesy of Colorado Preservation Inc.*

Dale's father, L.G. Maple, refused to make any comments to the press, but according to J. Edgar Hoover, L.G. Maple told the FBI on February 17—when son Dale was still at large, whereabouts unknown—that he had two loaded guns and wouldn't hesitate to use them if the two escaped prisoners showed up in San Diego.[44]

## 2

# Prison Camps

Maple's weekend in the prisoner compound in January 1944 wasn't an isolated breach in the security-lacking camp of the 620th. Another outlandish bit of duplicity had just occurred less than a month earlier, over New Year's Eve weekend, when from the evening of December 31, 1943, until the morning of January 3, while citizens and tourists of the Denver area enjoyed the holiday, a Nazi soldier from Rommel's Afrika Korps, clad in the uniform of a U.S. Army private, roamed freely in their midst.

Private Siering provided the clothes, funds and transportation for holiday mirth-making in the Denver area for a prisoner of war named Erhard Schwichtenberg. Schwichtenberg had inveigled Siering to take him somewhere to flee the ennui of the prison stockade. Siering agreed and even brought his wife along, although she was told that Schwichtenberg was an American soldier. Incredibly, if that wasn't enough, Siering left Schwichtenberg alone on New Year's Eve, with no supervision, based on his promise not to escape. The trusty Schwichtenberg checked into a hotel under a fictitious name, kept his word and later rejoined Siering, who eventually got him back to his prison camp without attracting attention.

After a thorough investigation, the army concluded the New Year's Eve escapades were designed to relieve a prisoner's boredom, nothing more, without "a scrap of evidence" to the contrary. Schwichtenberg, the army noted, did not contact enemy agents during his holiday weekend, nor did he make any telephone calls, suspicious or otherwise. The investigators knew this because the hotel was not a pay station and the hotel charges showed no telephone calls. The army admitted that no one knew how Schwichtenberg got out of the prisoner compound or how he returned. A subsequent search revealed that prisoners kept many articles of U.S. Army clothing in their barracks. In his subsequent interview with military investigators, Schwichtenberg remarked that he enjoyed his Denver holiday retreat. "I have," he proudly proclaimed, "seen beautiful America."[45]

## A Raft of Attempted Escapes

The U.S. government couldn't go after escaped prisoners of war once they got over the border into Mexico. At that point, the army hoped Mexican authorities would turn the prisoners over, for the going rate of twenty-five dollars a head. Along the border at the beginning of 1944, several prisoners had recently escaped, including from camps in Dallas; Fort Sill, Oklahoma; and Camp Alvin, Texas. March 1 brought news, courtesy of the *El Paso Herald-Post*, that authorities arrested a rancher sixty miles south of Juárez for employing two Italian prisoners who skipped out of an El Paso camp six months earlier. Of course, the rancher said he didn't know about any of that. The *American* (Odessa, Texas) carried an article on March 3 entitled "Nazi Prisoners Using Ingenious Methods in Trying to Escape from Camps in This Area." Five prisoners escaped from the Mexia Camp. All were recaptured within a day, three of them along the road at 2:15 a.m. A rural postal carrier noticed them and immediately contacted authorities.

The articles and blurbs from the old newspapers eerily resemble the runaway indentured servants mentioned in newspaper notices of the eighteenth century. So and so is a carpenter by trade and has a scar on his left arm. This one knows the printing trade and that one coppersmithing. This one doesn't speak English and that one may be heading to Baltimore, where his uncle lives.

In reality, the percentage of prisoners who attempted to escape was very small; some historians claim it was less than the escape rate of the general prison population. But even if only 1 percent of the prisoners departed camp, the authorities would have been searching for about 4,350 escapees. The escapes started as soon as the prisoners got to the United States. Newspaper notices of prisoners escaping were practically a daily occurrence, especially by late 1944. You would be hard pressed to *not* find a news account of an attempted prisoner of war escape on any day during the last year of the war, even after V-E Day in May 1945.

Sometimes there were two or more newspaper accounts on the same day. On May 24, 1945, for example, readers learned a prisoner escaped from a pulpwood detail in Camden, North Carolina, and two more from a Houston camp. Another day brought news that a prisoner had escaped for the third time, and several prisoners used the dummies-in-the-beds trick to buy themselves a little extra time. One incorrect blurb mentioned a prisoner's jacket had "WP" on the back, when in fact the letters were "PW." It's doubtful the typo lessened the public interest in locating said prisoner. Another reported that the two prisoners, eighteen and forty-six, who skipped out of the medical aid unit of a Mississippi camp, had "PP" stenciled on their clothes, which was not a typo, as they were considered Protective Personnel. In Nebraska, six prisoners were "captured" as they cut the fence to *re-enter* their own prison camp, complaining about the awful Nebraska weather. The grass wasn't any greener nor the air any warmer. Three escaped in June 1944 from Camp Concordia, Kansas, in the chaos following a tornado. A prisoner who escaped from an Oklahoma camp was overheard saying he wanted to get to another camp in time to celebrate his birthday.

One historian tabulated the number of prisoner escapes nationwide went from eighty-one in 1943, when the prisoners were just arriving in the United States, to a little more than a thousand during the entire year of 1944, to about three per day in 1945. Nineteen prisoners tried to escape from Camp Stark, New Hampshire, in one month, leading the *Berlin (New Hampshire) Reporter* to comment: "With six such escapes within a little over a week, surely the authorities themselves should be on the alert to put an end to the stop-and-scoot practices of the Germans at Stark."[46]

Stark's most famous escape featured a twenty-seven-year-old English-speaking prisoner who made his way to New York City, where he sold paintings in Central Park. To stem the escapes, the Stark prison commander established a unique system based on trust. In return for promising not to escape, the prisoners enjoyed greater latitude when they worked in town. They were subject to less security and scrutiny; guards did not have to constantly monitor them. They kept their promise with the understanding that they could later revoke that promise if they desired. Almost all gave their pledge and very few later revoked it.[47]

Twelve prisoners fled Camp Berkeley, near Abilene at the end of March 1944 through a sixty-foot tunnel. All were soon recaptured.[48] Three prisoners escaped from Camp Crossville, Tennessee, and came across a woman with a gun, who fired at them. When she heard they were Germans, she cried; she said she thought they were Yankees. Two prisoners escaped from a camp at

Scotts Bluff, Nebraska, in July 1944 and wandered through the United States and Canada for four months before eventually being captured from empty oil drums on a merchant ship. An escapee from Camp Grant escaped by hiding in dirty laundry. He got a job at a farm where he was arrested several months later. Two men simply walked out of Camp Somerset, Maryland, in U.S. Army uniforms in October 1945. They were arrested in New York six months later.

Historian Arnold Krammer, whose research and writing about prisoners of war is considered the gold standard, calculated that about two-thirds of escapees went through, over or under stockade fences to escape; the remaining simply walked away from their worksites. Fifty-six escaping prisoners were shot as they escaped.[49]

Reinhold Pabel escaped from a camp near Peoria, Illinois, in September 1945 and got picked up by a farmer as he hitchhiked outside the camp. In those days, with tire and gas rationing, it was considered patriotic to pick up hitchhikers. Pabel walked into a Social Security office and applied for a Social Security number under a fictitious name. He filed a tax return under

POWs working in a shop. *Courtesy of the Mississippi Armed Forces Museum–Birdsong Collection.*

the fictitious name, got a tax refund and married an American. Their first child was born in 1952. He frequently saw his picture on the Wanted posters at the post office. In March 1953, Pabel's mother-in-law convinced him to turn himself in. He later recounted his eight years on the loose in *Colliers*, in a story called "It's Easy to Bluff Americans."

A prisoner who escaped from Camp Butner, North Carolina, in 1945 became a model citizen. Almost fourteen years later, in May 1959, he turned himself in, saying that as a fugitive, he always felt under pressure. He was allowed to leave the United States voluntarily so he could reenter as a regular immigrant and apply for citizenship. Finally, Georg Gaertner, who escaped from Camp Deming, New Mexico, in September 1945 and lived for the next *forty* years under various aliases, turned himself in to the FBI in 1985.[50]

## Prisoners

By May 1942, there were only thirty-two prisoners of war interned in the United States. In August 1942, Great Britain requested the United States take and hold within one month 50,000 British-captured prisoners and take an additional 100,000 prisoners within three months. The United States agreed, but the expected influx of 1942 didn't materialize. By April 1943, fewer than 5,000 prisoners had arrived; by mid August 1943, however, the number had increased to more than 130,000.[51]

In all during the war, approximately 435,000 foreign soldiers were held in the United States as prisoners of war, spread out in about 660 installations, in every state except Vermont and Nevada. Housed in old Civilian Conservation Corps (CCC) barracks, national guard camps, air bases and numerous other locations where the government owned or purchased land and buildings, the 379,000 Germans, 51,000 Italians and 5,000 Japanese each received at least ten cents per day (officers got more) in canteen credits to buy beer, tobacco, candy and toiletries. They were paid in script: small tickets in denominations of one, five, ten, twenty-five and fifty cents.

U.S. guidelines required the camps be at least 170 miles from the ocean, at least 150 miles from Mexico or Canada, fewer than 5 miles from a railroad line and more than 500 feet from any public road.[52] By the end of the war, prison camps were allowed anywhere except near critical industries, such as munitions plants, and within a 10-mile radius of the White House, except for Andrews Field. The camps provided at least 120 square feet for officers, 40 for non-officers.

Originally, prisoners stayed in their compounds, tending gardens, reading and writing letters and playing cards. With the labor shortage in the United States, however, it wasn't long before the army started a program allowing prisoners to work in local communities. Captured officers could not be compelled to work outside the camps; enlisted men had no choice.

In April 1942, the army published "Civilian Enemy Aliens and Prisoners of War," the U.S. government's first interpretation of the Geneva Convention. The Geneva Convention, relative to the treatment of prisoners of war, entered into effect in 1931.

After a few changes, the War Department published in January 1943 "War Department Policy with Respect to Labor of Prisoners of War," which stated prisoners could do any work outside of combat zones that:

- didn't directly relate to war operations,
- didn't involve the manufacture or transportation of arms or munitions,
- didn't involve the transportation of material intended for combat units, and
- wasn't unhealthy, dangerous, degrading, or beyond the particular prisoner's physical capacity.[53]

Each country set its own guidelines to interpret the treaty's vague terms, such as unhealthy, dangerous and degrading. The prisoners performed all types of nonmilitary labor, virtually any job that had to be done. They harvested crops, built roads and waterways, felled trees, roofed barns, dug trenches, erected silos, constructed tract housing and baled hay. The auto industry used oil from tung nuts to prevent rust and reduce friction on engine parts, so prisoners picked tung nuts at plantations on the Mississippi Gulf Coast. They worked in laundries, mosquito control, soil conservation and strip mining. They operated ice plants, cleaned streets and poured concrete. In the last three months of 1943, prisoners picked more than six and a half million pounds of seed cotton in Mississippi, and in Maine during 1945, they harvested almost five million bushels of potatoes.[54]

Prisoners worked around the clock for a few days in May 1943 and 1944 packing sandbags against flood waters. Forty Italians set up a shoe repair shop at Camp Weingarten, Missouri. With no cobbler experience, they learned on the job and ended up repairing three to four hundred pairs of army shoes each day.[55]

POWs earned eighty cents a day for working in the communities. *Courtesy of Ricky Robertson Collection.*

For working in the communities, prisoners received eighty cents a day and officers a little more. Whoever hired them paid the prevailing labor rate with the excess over eighty cents per day going to the U.S. government. As of June 1945, the government had earned about $22 million by hiring prisoners out. As late as February 1945, congressional representatives were pressuring the military to bring over to America an additional 100,000 prisoners to relieve the farm labor shortage. All through the war, conflicts occurred about putting prisoners to work. With the exception of unions, most groups were on the side of using this source of labor. Organized labor, however, feared prisoners would take jobs from Americans. Congressman Jennings Randolph of West Virginia introduced a bill in the spring of 1945 prohibiting any federal agency from using prisoners for any skilled work.

Community and business leaders aggressively lobbied the army to establish camps in their towns. Camps meant an economic infusion of federal money, a great deal of it. Buildings had to be built, roofed, wired and painted. Water and drainage pipes had to be constructed and streets paved. Employees had to be hired to run and maintain the camps—no simple, small or inexpensive task. In addition, the service men and women brought into

POWs making concrete blocks. *Courtesy of the Mississippi Armed Forces Museum–Birdsong Collection.*

town to operate the camps wanted to eat out and be entertained and had the money to do so. The camps represented a gold rush bonanza of well-paying jobs and customers with money to spend. The prisoners couldn't spend their scrip in town, so the army set up savings accounts to help them save it for the end of the war. Script leftover or saved got converted into cash for the prisoners. In finalizing its accounts after the war, the U.S. government paid out $274,771,389.60 to the prisoners or their dependents for the value of unused canteen credits.[56]

Approximately 2,800 prisoners (1 Japanese, 600 Italians and 2,200 Germans) attempted to escape. The vast majority were apprehended within a couple days. In Arizona, German prisoners dug a tunnel, 180 feet long, where 25 of them made their break the day before Christmas in 1944. Six were recaptured immediately. The remaining nineteen were recaptured shortly after notices ran in the newspapers showing pictures of the men and offering a reward for their recapture. The worse recorded crime committed by a prison escapee was car theft. Several

POWs paving a road. *Courtesy of the Mississippi Armed Forces Museum–Birdsong Collection.*

reports mentioned that civilians, not prisoners, were the real concern: "The biggest problem is not to keep prisoners from making advances to people. The problem is to keep the people from fraternizing with prisoners—feelings of sympathy being manifested by attempts to give gifts….Most trouble…is caused by the civilian element rather than a failure of prisoners to observe rules and regulations."[57]

In Fairfax County, Virginia, approximately 200 German prisoners were stationed at a camp on Route 29. At the time, Fairfax County was the third-largest dairy producing county in the United States. The first prisoner arrived in Fairfax in June 1945, and the last one left in November 1945. In those five months, prisoners worked a total of 111,000 hours at almost 200 different farms around the county. Altogether, the State of Virginia held approximately seventeen thousand prisoners in twenty-seven installations.[58]

## WOMEN IN THE ESCAPE MIX

Several newspapers in 1948 picked up a series of columns by a reporter named Douglas Larsen concerning prisoners of war who were still on the loose. The articles sounded like a plea for help from the FBI or the military but were written as human interest stories. With the title "FBI Seeks Femme Angle in Tracking POWs," the notices placed much blame of escaped prisoners on women, who "figured prominently in the escape plots and are now playing a big part—knowingly or otherwise" in sheltering some or all of the sixteen German and two Italian prisoners still at large three years after the war.[59] The wife of a wealthy Mississippi cotton planter deserted her husband and family and ran away with a prisoner of war, at least for two days until they were picked up in a tourist camp. Two girls in Owosso, Michigan, narrowly averted a treason charge for their role in aiding two prisoners' escape. They had previously worked with the prisoners at a canning factory.

A prisoner named Rudolph Josef Soelch, twenty-four, identified in the newspapers as a former bodyguard of Herman Goering, escaped in April 1945 from Camp Haan, California, with the aid of James and Joan McBride, forty and forty-two, respectively. Previously, the McBrides had each been imprisoned for violations of California's Subversive Organization Registration Act, which essentially required people suspected by the government of disloyalty to register with the government. Mr. and Mrs. McBride hopped a train in California with Soelch and made it back to their home in Detroit where she got Soelch a job as a busboy and baker in the restaurant where she worked. An alert customer contacted authorities once he noticed the busboy looked just like the photo of an escaped prisoner on a Wanted poster. Soelch got deported forthwith; the McBrides got four years.[60]

In January 1948, Gloria Sammartino, twenty-five, of Winthrop, Massachusetts, was arrested for helping Rudolph von Hyeburg escape from a camp in Fort Devens, Massachusetts. They had met at the army hospital in Waltham, where she was a cook and he a kitchen helper. After his escape in 1946, he immediately boarded a train to New York and started using the surname of a man he read about in that day's newspaper obituary.[61] She was charged with harboring an escaped prisoner, not treason, meaning this came after April 30, 1945, the date Congress passed Public Law 47, making it a specific crime for aiding or harboring prisoners. Before that law, those arrested for aiding prison escapes were sometimes charged with treason.

In mid-November 1945, five residents of Dauphin County, Pennsylvania, were apprehended for helping two prisoners escape. Specifically, it was alleged, the residents let prisoners stay at their farm for nine days after their escape.[62]

A forty-five-year-old woman named Fannie Welvaert, mother of three sons and a daughter, all in the U.S. armed forces, helped prisoner Horst Becker escape in September 1945. She had been separated from her husband. Mrs. Welvaert and Becker were arrested two months later in Leominster, Massachusetts, on a charge of lewd and lascivious cohabitation. She was charged with aiding an escape and harboring a prisoner of war. She pled guilty in January 1946.[63]

An escape story catching a lot of interest involved three Japanese American sisters assigned to the Granada Relocation Center in southern Colorado. They helped two prisoners escape from the camp in Trinidad, Colorado, in October 1943. The Shitara sisters (Tsuruko "Toots" Wallace, Florence "Flo" Shivze Otani and Billie Shitara Tanigoshu), each in her thirties, had been relocated to Colorado from their home in a Los Angeles suburb. They had originally met and gotten to know the prisoners while working on the same farm. Using their own car, the sisters drove the prisoners about eighty-seven miles south of Trinidad, which was as far as they could get before their car broke down. The sisters got back home, and the prisoners walked the remaining miles to their first destination—the northern New Mexico town of Watrous. In addition to the car ride, the sisters provided clothes and money. The prisoners were quickly apprehended, and the sisters arrested, indicted and convicted for conspiracy to commit treason. Although they were later acquitted of the treason charge, these "little Benedict Arnolds," as the prosecution called them, subsequently spent two years in prison. A couple years later, in December 1946, one of the prisoners, back in Germany after the war, wrote to the judge asking for the names and addresses of the women so he could "beg the pardon for all the heartbreak we inflicted upon them at the time." The prisoner also asked for some food "of that nice American type."[64]

All of this is to illustrate the regularity of attempted escapes and, in many cases, the efforts to get to Mexico. In his report to Congress for fiscal year 1944, John Edgar Hoover reported the FBI's efforts in searching for and capturing escaped prisoners had increased sharply. During that period, the FBI stated no fewer than 410 prisoners had attempted to escape. Most were apprehended in a day or two, but four were still at large as of June 30, 1944. The fiscal year 1945 report cited 1,607 attempted escapes with 22 still at large as of June 30, 1945.[65]

Various numbers get kicked around regarding the number of prison escapes. A provost marshal's report from 1949 advised *New Yorker* writer E.J.

POWs baking bread. *Courtesy of the Mississippi Armed Forces Museum–Birdsong Collection.*

Kahn that all but fifteen Germans and one Italian had been recaptured. The Italian, the army knew, made it back to Italy, but military and government authorities chose to not pursue the matter.[66]

Escaping became easier in February 1944, when the army instituted a "calculated risk" policy, loosening security on the assumption that most prisoners wouldn't try to escape. General George Marshall wrote on December 1, 1942: "The business of guarding could be carried out on a limited basis and the escape of a few prisoners would not be too bad in its effect."[67] Army personnel, after all, were desperately needed for the war effort, not to guard prisoners who in reality weren't likely to escape. They had nowhere to go. As one later rhetorically asked, "who wants to go to Germany in wartime?" The prisoners weren't considered dangerous. If they escaped the army or FBI could quickly round them up. Most camps were specifically located in isolated areas, primarily in southern and western states. The prisoners had no cash (one of the reasons the army paid them in script not cash) and most didn't speak English.

# Fritz Ritz

Most of the prisoners didn't want to escape. They were treated well in camp, thanks to the Geneva Convention. Many Americans who lived near the camps, often referred to as "Fritz Ritz," thought prisoners had it too easy and were pampered. The prisoners were fed well. Indeed, the prisoners were the first to admit they had it good. Letter after letter reveals the prisoners' wonderment and appreciation for the quality and quantity of goods they were given. Their letters often mentioned they never ate so well in their entire military careers. They didn't have to suffer through shortages and rationing of butter, meat and other foods. They wrote about how comfortable they were and how they were provided with whatever they needed. While the rest of the world dealt with food shortages, one prisoner noted the prisoners could line their soccer fields with flour.[68]

The following two prisoners' experiences were not at all unusual:

> *We landed in Norfolk, Virginia where we showered and got deloused. They blew this pink powder all over our bodies. They boiled our clothes in a big steam kettle. Some guy said, "Throw everything away. Throw everything away. You get everything new in America." And we did. Everyone got a brand-new quilted blanket, two packs of cigarettes, an army razor and a can of Spam. That was our nice welcome to America. Nobody ever mistreated me in America. Not once did I get hit or verbally abused.*[69]

> *Upon entering the camp, we reported to clerks who filled out forms with our personal data and took our fingerprints. We had to take off our uniforms. Everything, including shoes and underwear, was thrown away. I was allowed to keep my wedding ring, a picture of my dear wife, and my belt, which I still wear to work today. We received new underwear, new socks, new shirts, and new green uniforms like those the Americans wore. The only difference was that a large PW was printed on every sleeve and pant leg and on the back of shirts and jackets. The hats also had PW printed in white. Now we all looked like P.O.W.s. It was a bit painful, but we were amazed that everything we got was new and that it fit well. Even the shoes were new and of the proper size. We also got toothpaste, a toothbrush, soap, towels, and even a handkerchief. We were all quite excited.*[70]

An article of the Geneva Convention stated prisoners should be provided with intellectual diversions and sports organizations, so the prisoners built theaters, soccer fields, workshops. They enjoyed libraries with books in English and German, as well as popular magazines. Each camp published its own newspaper, sometimes multiple newspapers. According to Arnold Krammer's *Nazi Prisoners of War in America*, an Arkansas camp boasted more than nine thousand books, and the musical schedule for a single camp in Mississippi for the month of July 1944 reveals eight separate performances, including some by a twenty-member brass orchestra for audiences of up to 960 per performance. The prisoners carved wood, took classes, sculpted, painted and gardened. The camp's soccer teams competed in tournaments against other camps. A prisoner from an Alabama camp recalled:

> *Sports started right after breakfast, and our camp had a whole slate of outstanding teams in soccer, handball, volleyball, etc. Athletic activities were taken very, very seriously. The camp championships, especially in soccer and handball, were so exciting that even our guards participated as cheerleaders from their towers and attended the games on weekends with their families shouting from the sidelines. Many of our athletes, as a matter of fact, went on to sports careers in Germany after their release.*[71]

The biggest source of resentment against prisoners might have come from the fact that although the prisoners kept busy with their hobbies, they originally did nothing to benefit either the local communities or the United States. The decision to employ prisoners came slowly, with controversy and bureaucratic delays. The United States didn't have any experience with handling hundreds of thousands of foreign prisoners. In World War I, a historian noted, the United States held only 1,346 prisoners.[72]

The *New York Times Magazine* featured an article on November 21, 1943, titled, "Nazi Prisoners Are Nazis Still." The article charged that prisoners were "better off with food than average citizens on the outside. They have no rationing troubles and no shortages of anything." The reporter observed in the prisoners' kitchens "piles of juicy hams, plenty of butter, steaks, and sausages."[73]

Widely respected newspaper columnist Walter Winchell railed early and often against the army's coddling, complaining the prisoners wandered about town without guards and were treated as war heroes. Columnist Drew Pearson complained: "German prisoners of war, many of them arrogant, insolent, and considered beyond political rehabilitation, get rationed foods denied civilians, and in some cases receive scarce foods requiring four times the food stamps now allowed American civilians."[74]

The *Saturday Evening Post* published an article on March 3, 1945, called "Are We Coddling Italian Prisoners?" *Collier's* repeatedly brought the issue up; a story in its October 14, 1944 issue was titled "Our Pampered War Prisoners." The *United States News* on January 29, 1945, ran a story titled "Are Prisoners Pampered?" The *Courier-News* of Plainfield, New Jersey, asked:

> *Why should former prisoners be molly-coddled? They killed or help kill our boys. When they were defeated at the cost of our blood and sweat they threw up their hands and surrendered. Then we take them on picnics…the Brass Hats of the War Department (or whoever is responsible) are carrying it too far when they give war prisoners the "key to the city" and permit them to be taken on sight-seeing picnics and tours. The next thing we know, we'll have Mussolini, Hitler, and Tojo touring the country as our guests.*[75]

Americans condemned the apparent coddling, especially of Italian prisoners of war who, after Italy surrendered in September 1943, had much more freedom than German prisoners. Italian prisoners were declared "co-belligerents" and organized into Italian Service Units, removing many of the restrictions of the Geneva Convention. They were still considered prisoners, but barely.

American soldiers in Virginia Beach, according to the *Washington Post*, were "fed up with the Italians strolling along the boardwalk and flirting with the bathing beauties….Enlisted Italians serving in army service units in this country are living up to the adage about Latins being romantically inclined by yelling 'Hello, Gorgeous' and walking away with the GI girls on furlough."[76]

*Business Week* opined: "These Italians have reached a captive's utopia, enjoying all of military life's necessities and a few of the privileges denied their skulking comrades and their erstwhile allies from Germany."[77]

The *Boston Herald* complained on February 12, 1945, about providing Italian prisoners with musical instruments, arranged dances, hundreds of pounds of Italian pasta, bocce balls and operatic recordings. The newspaper opined that making heroes out of prisoners, who "are our guests only by virtue of having shot it out on the battlefield with American kids and lost… is a queer way of adding up the score."[78]

The *Chicago Tribune* reported on August 18, 1944, that "rock-wielding Negro troops" attacked sleeping members of an Italian Service Unit in their barracks at Fort Lawton, Seattle, killing one prisoner and injuring twenty-four. An altercation between white American soldiers and the Italian prisoners had occurred a day before the barracks raid. Many American troops deeply resented the coddling of Italian soldiers and felt they were given easier work

POWs took classes, some sponsored by colleges. *Courtesy of Ricky Robertson collection.*

than members of the Negro post battalion. Among other complaints, they resented the army taking the Italians on tours to baseball games and parks.

Conditions got worse for German prisoners in the spring of 1945 following V-E Day. The prisoners' diets were severely restricted. All meals were smaller and not nearly as good. Recreation programs got cut or eliminated, correspondence was tightened or restricted, the pay for nonworking noncommissioned officers was significantly reduced and prisoners could no longer use canteen coupons for beer, candy bars or cigarettes. In addition, prisoners' work quotas were raised. And to show the army wasn't coddling prisoners, it started assigning returning American prisoners of war to guard the prisoners, the idea being those American guards would be especially tough on prisoners, having formerly been prisoners themselves. Surprisingly, it didn't work out as planned. The returning American prisoners were probably kinder than the previous guards, perhaps because they understood the plight of the prisoners. These new guards empathized with the prisoners they were now assigned to guard. By the end of 1945, the pendulum swung back. Life in camp lightened up again and many of the restrictions were removed.

The coddling allegation was a very politically sensitive topic. Many thought the prisoners were pampered, but many others understood, then and now, the reasons and benefits of treating prisoners well. It was the right thing to do, and it conformed with the Geneva Convention. Sarah Vowell's book called *Assassination Vacation* has a great line on the subject: "The day a person gives up on the Geneva Convention is the day a person gives up on the human race." The army's philosophy during the war was that by treating prisoners well, word would get to Europe and would hopefully prompt the Germans to treat their captured American prisoners well. Indeed, there is an abundance of evidence indicating this occurred. In addition, word of

Prisoners put on musical performances in camp. *Courtesy of Camp Hearne Collection & Exhibit, Hearne, Texas.*

the good treatment would spur more Germans to surrender. On August 12, 1944, the editors of *Collier's* opined:

> *We ought to be humane and generous in this matter because we are Americans, and because we have always believed as a nation in decency, humanity, humaneness and a break for the underdog—which war prisoners certainly are. If we should take to maltreating war prisoners, we would betray something fine in our national make-up; and the consequences of that betrayal would kick back in our own teeth.*[79]

## DANGER

*The degree of civilization in a society can be judged by entering its prisons.*
*—Fyodor Dostoyevsky*

The most danger that prisoners posed was to fellow prisoners in the same camp, those considered "stool pigeons" and those considered soft on Nazism.

One of them, Werner Drechsler, was murdered by Papago Park's ardent Nazis on March 12, 1944, within a few hours of arriving at the Phoenix camp. The seven Nazi prisoners charged, convicted and executed for his murder constitute perhaps the last mass execution by the U.S. government. The seven were hanged one at a time in August 1945 over a period lasting approximately two and a half hours. The *Fort Leavenworth News* carried a description that boasted a new system for mass hangings that saved more than an hour in the procedure. A month earlier another seven prisoners of war had been hanged at Fort Leavenworth, two of them for murdering a fellow prisoner at a camp in Aiken, South Carolina, and five for murdering a fellow prisoner at Camp Gruber, Oklahoma. Several other prisoners, at various times during the war, were also executed for crimes against fellow prisoners.[80]

# 3

# Escape

In the late morning of Tuesday, February 15, 1944, prisoners Erhard Schwichtenberg and Heinrich Kikillus walked about one hundred yards from their stockade, down an embankment of approximately thirty feet, to a car parked by the side of the road with the driver pretending to be repairing the car. It was never revealed whether any U.S. Army soldiers or WACs helped the prisoners leave their stockade or exactly how the message was passed notifying them when and where to meet with someone pretending to be repairing an automobile. The prisoners later claimed they didn't know ahead of time the identity of the driver or the model of the car. Dale Maple claimed he did not know which prisoners would show up for the escape. The escape had been planned for at least several weeks, with the original stratagem having eight prisoners escaping in two cars, each car driven by a soldier from the 620th. However, an American soldier's reluctance to get mixed up in the perfidy forced the plan's downsizing to just one American driver escaping with four prisoners, which in the end got reduced to two for reasons lost to history. It's hard to believe more would not have tried, given there was no penalty against them for attempting to escape.

Maple later said the departure was hastened by a credible rumor that the army was about to transfer the 620th, ostensibly to a location with greater security and restrictions. Maple took a short post-jentacular walk from his job on the sawmill detail on February 15, falsely claiming he was going to sick call. He got in his car, which he was not allowed to own, and departed with the two prisoners, whom he was not allowed to associate with. The car had been packed the night before with rucksacks for Maple and four prisoners. Maple later testified the rucksacks had been filled by prisoners.

Maple worked on base as an electrician, but he had been assigned—demoted—a week earlier to the sawmill detail, the least desirable assignment in camp. He believed the demotion was a penalty for assisting another soldier—Fritz Loock—in an effort to try to get out of the army by claiming an illegal enlistment. Maple's transfer to the sawmill detail came a day after Loock refused to obey a direct order.

## FRITZ LOOCK

*Fritz Loock was a German citizen serving in the 620th. Since age fourteen, Fritz Willy Heinrich Loock had been at sea. In August 1939, he walked into Bayonne, New Jersey, from a docked ship, entering the United States illegally. He was a mess steward on the* Franz Klasen, *of the Waried Line, a subsidiary of the Standard Oil Company. He simply liked New York and wanted to stay. All his family were back in Germany, and he had a brother in the German navy. He claimed he later tried to return to Germany but was prevented because of the war. He lived in hotels in New York City until the FBI arrested him in 1941 and detained him at Ellis Island for four months. After his release from Ellis Island in September 1941, he worked as a tinsmith until being inducted in the U.S. Army in August 1943. But he wasn't really inducted, having turned his back and walked away as the oath was read to him and the other inductees.*

*Those who had done the swearing in of tens of thousands of men required to serve because of the draft, often didn't care whether a man didn't raise his hand, or didn't swear an oath to serve. They didn't care whether the person was a U.S. citizen or whether he belonged in the military. Their job was to get those men into the ranks and into uniform. Others could sort it out later. There was no upside to them for dealing with matters like this. There was a war to be fought. A man contesting his citizenship or arguing he didn't belong in the military was ignored and before he knew it, despite his protestations, he was in uniform, serving in the U.S. military.*

*Loock's court-martial file includes several letters objecting to service in the U.S. Army. He answered the question "I do not object to service in the Armed Services of the United States" by scratching out the word "not." But no one in the army cared whether Loock legally belonged in the army. There was a draft, and he was drafted. Another one of his letters stated: "As an alien of*

Fortuitously for Maple, a note posted on the 620th bulletin board on Monday night, February 14, stated that Alexander Altman, the soldier in charge of the sawmill detail, would be going to the dental infirmary the next morning. Altman's regular replacement on the sawmill duty when he wasn't in charge happened to be Paul Kissman, a good friend of Maple's. As expected, Kissman substituted for Altman on Tuesday morning, and like the loyal friend and disgruntled private that Kissman was, he looked the other way when Maple departed camp for the Mexican border. When Altman

*German birth I will under no circumstances serve in the armed forces of the United States. I am in this country against my will and hope this finds your kind understanding." His letters culminated on February 6, 1944, when he refused any further military service until his wife was released from internment or until he was interned with her. She had been in the country since 1939, and they were married in 1940. She had been detained since November 1943 as an enemy alien–first at Ellis Island and later at Crystal City, Texas–due to her German nationality.*

*As threatened, the next day, February 7, Loock disobeyed a direct order to go to work on the sawmill detail. He was court-martialed, found guilty of the Article of War 64 and sentenced to three years of hard labor at Fort Leavenworth. In his court-marital trial, the only defense witness was Loock himself, who tried to explain that he ended up in the army through mishaps and errors.*

*According to the court-martial files, Loock did not come up with his defiance plan on his own. A note in Loock's file states, with the underlining, "Pvt Loock was a friend of <u>Dale Maple</u>." In fact, Maple had given Loock advice on the morning Loock disobeyed the direct order. Maple suggested that Loock use the courts to get his discharge. Loock testified only that Maple didn't try to dissuade him from his plan to disobey.*

*Within a few months, the army came to agree with Loock. A decision in a U.S. Supreme Court case vacated Loock's court-martial sentence. The army couldn't court-martial and imprison someone who wasn't ever legally inducted in the army. The army recommended Loock be released from confinement, receive a blue discharge and then be interned in a civilian camp. A blue discharge entitled him to hospitalization and domiciliary care by the Veterans' Administration. Under the circumstances, the report added, it seemed unjust to give him a dishonorable discharge.*

returned from his dental appointment at about 1:00 p.m., he learned from Kissman that Maple was at sick call. The disbelieving Altman immediately went to sick call to check and learned that Maple wasn't there and hadn't been there all day.

Weeks later, Kissman explained why he helped give Maple extra time by lying about the sick call. In a screed entitled "Why I Covered Maple's Escape Temporarily," Kissman listed nineteen complaints about the army and about tension in the 620th and the prison camp. He said those nineteen were just a few examples of the problems, the gist of his argument being that both soldiers and prisoners were all so bitter, angry and volatile that the escape was like a valve releasing hostilities. Tension had been building up among the prisoners about who would depart with Maple. "The best I could make out was that the rivalry among the prisoners as to who should go was becoming so bad that it might have broken out into the ranks; that the sooner they left, it would be better."[81]

Kissman, with his long philosophical rants, turgidly began one essay with the sentence, "The porcupines [*sic*] only defense is the quills" and ended another by saying that Maple, the man he intentionally covered for, was stubborn and stupid. Kissman called Maple's attempted escape a "worthless act" that neither he nor anyone else in the 620th condoned, comments rich in deceit given Kissman's involvement in purchasing in Denver a .38 Colt revolver and fifty rounds of ammunition for Maple's escape. He acquired the gun at Maple's behest and with Maple's money, and—for an added level of treachery and scienter—Kissman conducted the entire transaction through a third party *and* with a fictitious name.

Kissman and a soldier named Frederick Maurer also purchased two compasses for $5.00 at a pawnshop, a red-checkered cowboy shirt and a white shirt for $1.95 each, a coat and a sextant. Kissman and Maurer spent the weekend in Denver on this shopping trip before returning via a four-hour bus ride to Camp Hale at four in the morning on February 8. A few hours later, Kissman personally handed the gun and other items to Maple.

Maple and his Teutonic duo hit the road for Mexico in a ten-year-old used car, a 1934 Reo "Flying Cloud" that Maple had purchased a couple days earlier from Y&R Garage in Salida, Colorado, for $255 ($250 for the car plus $5 in tax). The first bump on the road trip: Maple had to simply drive off the base. Maple drove past the military police station several times, back and forth, making numerous U-turns, doing practically everything he could, he claimed, short of honking his horn to get noticed, all in the hopes

From here to the Mexican border is about six hundred miles. *Courtesy of the Tenth Mountain Division Resource Center, Denver Public Library.*

the military police would detain him. Getting stopped at any point on the trip, even before they departed camp, Maple claimed, would have sparked sufficient attention and publicity to him and to the plight of the 620th. But, alas, the MPs didn't notice, so the escapees had no choice but to drive on toward Mexico.

It was never explained why someone wanting to get caught would go to the trouble and expense of purchasing women's clothes to be used as a disguise, which Maple did the weekend before the escape. He later admitted the scarf and sweater were intended as a disguise for one of the prisoners. Since the purchase was made just before Valentine's Day, the merchant in Salida assumed Maple wanted the items gift wrapped.

At Bateman's Hardware shop, "Pat" Patterson struck up a friendly conversation with one of the two American soldiers who came into his store just as he was closing on February 12, 1944. He later remembered the conversation because one of the customers, the one looking but not buying, mentioned he had once worked in Newcastle, Pennsylvania. Patterson had also once worked in Newcastle. Patterson recalled the details later at Maple's court-martial trial. The soldier doing the buying—Maple—bought fishing gear, .22 cartridges and three sets of infantry insignia. The Colorado History Center has a glossy photograph of a dapper looking Patterson, who sent the photograph and a letter to *New Yorker* writer E.J. Kahn when Kahn was doing research for his 1950 magazine article. Patterson remarked in his letter to Kahn that he was the last living Salida merchant who had testified at Maple's trial.

Maple bought a man's hat, size 7 1/8, for $4.95. Weeks later, when the subject of the hat purchase came up at trial, however, the cashier at the Golden Rule Merchandising Company wasn't able to state with certainty who had purchased the hat or whether the hat shown to her at trial was the hat she sold to Dale Maple.

First stop on the trip after leaving Camp Hale was the town of Salida, about seventy miles away. The trio stopped at the Y&R Garage to pick up car license plates and a gas ration book. For reasons unknown to the author, these items were not provided to Maple when he bought the car. Fritz Owen, the counter employee at Y&R when Maple arrived at about 2:30 p.m., didn't know anything about anyone picking up tags and a gas ration book. Maple told him he was on furlough and in "sort of a hurry." Owen looked around and under the counter. He quickly found the items. He turned them over to Maple, who paid $9.85 and got back on the road. Owen noticed there were other people in the Reo.[82]

Maple was in a hurry, but little could he have known that it took more than a day for the prisoners' absence to be noted back in camp. An American soldier going AWOL was one thing and might not have attracted immediate attention; but going AWOL with two prisoners of war would set off alarms. Part of the delay in noticing the prisoners had fled resulted from a change in commander that day at the prison stockade. The regular commander had received a telegram the morning of February 15, ordering him to drop everything and head immediately to Camp Trinidad. His replacement, Second Lieutenant Robert Dawson, arrived in the early afternoon. Dawson later claimed the prisoners at the camp were all checked in, as usual, at 5:30 p.m. on the fifteenth, but no one noticed two of them missing. It wasn't until the next morning that someone realized Schwichtenberg and Kikillus weren't there. Dawson spent about three and a half hours on the morning of February 16 searching for the prisoners throughout the stockade and camp. He wanted to make absolutely sure they were really missing before he reported them missing. It wasn't until late Wednesday afternoon that the army reported a soldier and two prisoners had escaped. By that time, the escapees were well on their way to the border.

The escape itself and the secrecy and the urgency to get away quickly directly conflict with Maple's later assertions that he wanted to get caught. Why would someone wanting to be caught tell the counter man at Y&R Garage that he was in a hurry? Why would someone wanting to be caught take steps to conceal his escape? Perhaps Maple's claims about wanting to get caught were a lie. But then, perhaps, as Maple claimed, he really believed that getting caught in what appeared to be a sincere escape attempt would garner more publicity than a feeble attempt. All we have are written records. Maple's only statements about this were during his trial, when he had an incentive to lie to protect himself.

The travelers had a flat tire near Española, New Mexico, about thirty-five miles north of Santa Fe. They slept in their car. The next day, after the tire was repaired at a filling station, they drove through Santa Fe and Albuquerque to Hatch, New Mexico, on Highway 85. At about this point in the journey—it's not precisely clear when or where—they had another flat tire that they couldn't repair. So they continued driving on the rim with a flat tire. To help evade detection, they drove only at night and rested during daylight hours.

Along the way they passed near Bernalillo and Doña Ana, two towns they would see later. Turning southwest they headed to Deming, New Mexico, which increased the length of the trip but got them off the road where authorities would be expected to be looking for them. Except for about an hour, Maple did all the driving on the trip. Not much more of note happened until they got to Deming, where Maple drove the car off the road and into a ditch. Maple later claimed he intentionally drove into the ditch to attract attention and get detained, but alas, no matter how hard he tried he couldn't get anyone to arrest him. It didn't go unnoticed later, however, that contrary to his claims, Maple took evasive measures, such as getting off the main road to avoid detection, as the travelers got near the Mexican border. Someone wanting to be noticed wouldn't take clandestine actions to go unnoticed.

At about one thirty in the morning of February 17, an off-duty U.S. customs employee named John Breen saw the Reo in a ditch, about seven miles south of Deming. Breen was driving south from Deming to Columbus, and at this point, he had not heard anything about the escape. He pulled over to help. Breen talked to the man in the ditch standing outside the car. After some discussion about getting the car out of the ditch, Breen pulled his car, a 1942 Buick, bumper-to-bumper with the Reo. The bumpers lined up nicely, allowing Breen to push Maple's car far enough—about a hundred yards—to jump-start it. Maple was back on the road to Mexico, followed by an off-duty lawman who happened to also be heading south on the same road. Breen followed the Reo for seven or eight miles and eventually passed it, noting the driver of the car didn't turn the headlights on until Breen passed. During the pre-push discussion, Breen suspected something amiss. He observed what he thought were passengers in the car, a woman with a baby in her arms in the front seat and another person in back. But it was too dark to be sure. The lawman with twenty-four years' experience, however, suspected enough to write down the car's license tag number.

That might have been the end of the Breen connection except that about six hours later, on the very same road, Breen saw the Reo again. This time it was parked, empty and (unknown to Breen) out of gas, about seventeen miles from the Mexican border, about five to six miles farther south than where Breen passed it the night before. He double checked to confirm the Reo's license plate matched his scribbled notes from the night before.

A couple of hours earlier, when the Reo ran out of gas, the trio walked for a few miles before sleeping by the side of the road for the night. The next day, they hiked across the border and made it about two or three miles into Mexico, the apogee of their expedition, before being apprehended by Mejía. An army report later summarizing the case mentioned there was good reason to believe someone in Columbus, New Mexico, helped Maple get to Mexico, a lead the army didn't pursue, pointing out it was the FBI's jurisdiction to investigate civilians.[83]

# 4
# Jellybean and the Vagabond

As the special agent in charge of the El Paso FBI office, it was Delf "Jellybean" Bryce's job to know all about Nazis in America, saboteurs and prisoners' escapes. The El Paso office at that time covered much of west Texas as well as the entire state of New Mexico.

Bryce would later come into his own bit of national celebrity. Not many law enforcement agents were profiled with photos in *Life Magazine*, but that's what happened in November 1945 when America was introduced to Bryce and his shooting exploits. Titled "G-Man Can Draw a Gun Faster Than You Can Read This," the article reported Bryce's impressive feats, including one where the legendary lawman held a silver dollar with his shooting hand at forehead level, dropped the coin, and shot—and hit—the coin by the time it got to waist level. The *Life* photos showed a montage, slow motion–like, of Bryce doing this trick—stroboscopic photos they were called. Another photo showed a silhouette target with a tight circle in the middle of the chest. He could draw in two-fifths of a second and by aiming his body in a unique position and using the footwork of a basketball player, he would fall forward if hit, so he could keep on shooting. The *Life* editors concluded that Bryce was "the FBI agent most likely to live longest" and that he could have easily outdrawn western gunmen like Billy the Kid.[84]

Three months after the *Life* profile, a British magazine called *Picture Post* featured Bryce in a cover story titled "Quickest Man on the Draw":

*Delf Bryce is a G-man who can beat the pistol-packing criminal at his own game. He is quicker on the draw than any other F.B.I. agent, which is saying a lot, for G-manning America is not a* métier *in which you can take it easy and still go on living. He learned his stuff at the pistol-shooting course of the Federal Bureau of Investigation, after nine years in the Oklahoma police force. He is 39, and the best of some 4,000 experts on the lightning draw. Perhaps he had a natural quickness greater than that of any of the others, but it was long and painstaking practice that made him the first of the four thousand. The F.B.I. method allows only one count, in which the agent, with a swooping, circular movement, seizes his gun, draws it, aims and fires. He daren't fumble, for his man has been practising too—sometimes on other G-men who didn't live to say what went wrong. But, though the gangster doesn't hang around to have* his *speed measured, he must be pretty good to equal Mr. Bryce.*[85]

Delf Albert Bryce's nickname, "Jellybean," later shortened to Jelly, came through his affinity for wearing stylish threads. The jargon of the 1930s had a snappy dresser tagged as a jellybean. If you read about Special Agent Bryce—and there's plenty out there: the legendary

D.A. Bryce, "City Cop," 1932. *Courtesy of the Oklahoma Publishing Company Collection at the Oklahoma Historical Society.*

and indefatigable agent of epic and almost cartoonish proportions, prized gunsmith, personally handpicked to join the FBI by J. Edgar Hoover himself—you get the sense that if there was a Law Enforcement Hall of Fame, Bryce would have gone in with the first group of inductees.

Born on December 6, 1906, Bryce worked with the Oklahoma City Police Department from July 1928 until November 1934, when he became an FBI special agent. The FBI background investigation to determine his suitability for service included remarks by several FBI supervisors who interviewed Bryce, including one named Brantley who remarked that Bryce was from a good family and was part Indian. The aspects of

Special agent "Jelly" Bryce was handpicked by J. Edgar Hoover to join the FBI. *Courtesy of the Oklahoma Publishing Company Collection at the Oklahoma Historical Society.*

being a bit wild, unpolished and even uncouth, Brantley claimed, could be attributed to Bryce's youth, and in the long run, Bryce would make a better than average agent. Another supervisor noted Bryce appeared self-confident without being boastful. Bryce's application file notes he was an excellent shooter and that he had numerous victorious gun battles as an officer. There was one blemish on his record: In July 1928, he had punched Tex Burdett, the chief of police of Earlsboro, Oklahoma. But that was explained away because witnesses said the chief of police picked the fight.[86]

## Bryce Meets Maple

On February 19, 1944, Bryce must have suspected right away that something was very odd in the interview with the man calling himself Eduard Müeller. When Bryce entered the jail cell, Müeller snapped to attention, clicked his heels, gave the Nazi salute and shouted, "Heil Hitler!"[87]

It would have been no surprise to believe the three wanderers in Mexico were recent escapees from one of the prisoner of war camps near the border. Two days earlier, the *Globe-Times* had reported that four prisoners had escaped from the McLean camp, a little west of Amarillo. One of the four happened to be named Karl Müeller. The *El Paso Herald-Post* reported Agent Bryce was looking into the matter.

So Agent Bryce, who at that time was investigating the escape of a prisoner named Karl Müeller, had come across a man identifying himself as Eduard Müeller, who presented a prisoner of war identification card indicating he was a captured German soldier. With a heavy German accent, Eduard Müeller talked about his service in the German army. He said he had studied English as a child in Germany but that it was a long time ago.

Müeller kept up this Nazi impersonation and deceit for a while during the interview, conflicting accounts have it from one to three hours. Bryce later said the Nazi impersonation was perfect. Eventually, however, on that Friday afternoon, the charade ended and the ersatz Nazi admitted that everything he said during the interview up to that point had been a lie. He didn't have any German blood in him, didn't have family in Germany and had never been to Germany or, for that matter, anywhere overseas. He admitted his name was Dale H. Maple. As soon as Maple dropped the phony Eduard Müeller act and the German accent, Bryce terminated the interview. At 5:00 p.m. on February 19, Maple was arraigned on a charge of treason in federal court in Las Cruces, New Mexico, before U.S. commissioner Jess C. Williams. He pleaded not guilty, waived the preliminary hearing and was committed to the Bernalillo County Jail in Albuquerque in lieu of a $100,000 bond.

Bryce spent several subsequent days questioning the accused. Maple admitted all the details in the sordid saga, and with scripturient alacrity, he pounded out for Bryce a seven-thousand-word typed statement. Along with Maple and Bryce, four FBI agents signed the statement as witnesses.

None of the details of the affair could have had much affect on Bryce, for he had seen it all. Even the part about Maple getting hit by a car as a young boy wouldn't have meant much because Bryce had his own run-in with a near-deadly accident as a lad, having been the victim at age sixteen of a bullet fired from a rifle.

Maple revealed how he and his confederates strategized to destroy railroads and bridges throughout the United States. The plan fell through and eventually changed to a scheme where ten men in two cars would escape to Mexico, about six hundred miles away, fighting it out to the last man. Over time, the number of cars and participants decreased until it ended up as one army soldier and two prisoners making the run for the border, with plans to make contact in Chihuahua with an unnamed German agent; from there, they would head to Mexico City, where they would exchange for Mexican pesos the couple thousand francs in their possession. Then they would go to San Andrés, Tuxtla, Mexico, a seaport on the Gulf of Mexico, to meet a German family who lived on an island on a lake there, the only family living on the island. The father was a German agent, according to information from an American soldier in the 620th named Theophil Leonhard, who obtained the information from the former German counselor to Mexico, Von Kronenberg, who had several underground railroad contacts in Central and South America. Then they would head to Panama, where a boat would ferry them to Columbia, South America, to contact George Albert, ostensibly a representative of the Kaiser Textile Mills, who would help Maple and the prisoners get to Germany.[88]

The swastika flags that two of the escapees waved upon their apprehension in Mexico had nothing to do with vexillology or parades but were intended to show the men were escaped prisoners of war and not spies. Prisoners weren't penalized for trying to escape; spies were executed. The prisoners didn't want anyone to misunderstand.

Jelly demonstrating the shooting speed that made him a legendary lawman. *Courtesy of the Oklahoma Publishing Company Collection at the Oklahoma Historical Society.*

District Attorney Houk later said Maple admitted he was a gung-ho Nazi and had hoped to make his way, along with the two prisoners, to Germany to join Hitler's forces. History doesn't record whether Maple told Houk and Bryce that his family tree branched out to a couple of lawmen, including an uncle, Ralph Maple, who died in the line of duty. Dale Maple's grandfather George Maple was the police chief of Colton, California—sometimes he was referred to as the sheriff in the old newspaper articles—for a couple years until October 1917, when he resigned about a year after the tragic death of his son, Ralph Maple, twenty-seven, a special officer on the Colton force who was killed in the line of duty in September 1916 while attempting to make an arrest. On the day Ralph Maple died, the newspaper reported that Chief Maple didn't yet know about the shooting because he had just left town a few hours earlier for a vacation trip north and no one had been able to contact him.

On February 25, 1944, Houk turned over custody of Maple and jurisdiction for prosecution of the case to the War Department after being ordered to do so by the attorney general. The treason complaint filed in Albuquerque was dismissed without being presented to a federal grand jury. Agent Bryce's role in the matter would be limited to testifying as a witness at Maple's court-marital trial.

Jelly showing fourteen-year-old Billy Blair how to handle a rifle. *Courtesy of the Oklahoma Publishing Company Collection at the Oklahoma Historical Society.*

Dale Maple was charged with Articles of War 58 and 81.

> *Article 58: Desertion*
> *Any person subject to military law who deserts or attempts to desert the service of the United States shall, if the offense be committed in time of war, suffer death or such other punishment as a court-martial may direct, and, if the offense be committed at any other time, any punishment, excepting death, that a court-martial may direct.*
>
> *Article 81: Relieving, Corresponding With, or Aiding the Enemy*
> *Whosoever relieves or attempts to relieve the enemy with arms, ammunition, supplies, money, or other thing, or knowingly harbors or protects or holds correspondence with or gives intelligence to the enemy, either directly or indirectly, shall suffer death or such other punishment as a court-martial or military commission may direct.*[89]

Lasting five days and receiving testimony from twenty-six witnesses, the trial lacked controversy or fireworks. For the most part it reviewed facts and evidence already known. Maple supplied many of the details through his written statement two months earlier to Agent Bryce. Only Maple's intent and motives, not the facts, were disputed. At the trial's opening on April 24, 1944, Maple's mother, Mae C. Scoville, had already been in town for ten days, and Maple's father had just driven more than 1,900 miles in forty-nine hours, with only three hours' rest, to get to the trial in time. In setting the trial's ground rules, the three-man defense team (Humphrey Biddle, an attorney in private practice; Defense Counsel Rinold L. Ohman, a major in the cavalry; and Assistant Defense Counsel William Fleischaker, a second lieutenant) pushed hardest for their request to allow Maple's father, L.G. Maple, to assist and be allowed to sit at the defense table. The court said that decision was out of its hands; senior officers in Washington would decide. Biddle pointed out there was nothing in the court-martial manual limiting the number of defense counselors or requiring that counsel be an attorney, and in fact, one of the officers assigned by the army to defend Maple (Major Ohman) was not an attorney. Excluding Maple's parents, Biddle bellowed, would mean the trial represented, for the first time in the history of American criminal jurisprudence, an instance that the parents of a man charged with a capital offense had not been permitted to sit side by side with their son or at least in the same courtroom. Biddle made clear he wasn't trying to find fault with the court. "We are not trying to get anything by subterfuge. The father

Camp Hearne barracks, now the Visitor Center. *Courtesy of Camp Hearne Collection & Exhibit, Hearne, Texas.*

is deeply interested in the case." To the question of whether the rights of the accused would be prejudiced by excluding Maple's father from assisting the defense, Biddle responded, "Yes, sir. Emphatically, yes, sir." Biddle added:

> *The father has the whole background, not particularly the charges here, but the whole background of his son, and when the time comes, he will tell you about it. He should be sitting here helping his son, listening to the witnesses, and he himself should have the opportunity to cross-examine these witnesses. I just don't see how the—I mean this, of course, in the nicest way possible—that you can deny the accused the right to select his own counsel….He knows many things about this case that I for one do not, and I imagine that is about the same situation with Major Ohman and Lt. Fleischaker.*[90]

Dale Maple told the court that it was impossible for defense counsel to learn all about the case in a week. His parents were the only ones acquainted with him to know some of the facts of the matter. The court took a break

POW Camp Concordia reconstructed guardhouse. *Courtesy of Audrey Kalivoda.*

and returned with the decision from Washington: Maple's father could not be introduced as an associate defense counsel unless he was an attorney. Thus, L.G. Maple, who was not an attorney, would be treated like any other witness, to be examined and cross-examined in due course.

Other rules had to be worked out and notices made, such as emphasizing the offense charged was not treason because treason was a charge for civilian courts, not military court-martials. Several military reports, however, including at least one written after the trial, characterized the case as treason. Title 50, dealing with disclosure of secret or confidential matters, was read out loud in court. The prosecution noted the act was understood by court reporters, court members, all defense counsel, all trial judge advocates and all observers present in the court. There had been no formal extradition returning Maple from Mexico to the United States but no one raised this at the trial. Arrangements had to be made to get the Mexican customs officials to appear and testify in court.

While the prosecution cross-examined Dale Maple, inquiring about his prior statements to Agent Bryce, rapidly firing off a barrage of "didn't you say this" and "isn't it true you said that" questions, the flummoxed Biddle spoke up to get the questioning slowed, arguing he hadn't seen Maple's written statement—referred to as a confession—from which the prosecution was reading.

> *These questions are coming pretty fast. You are reading from something we have not seen. Give us a chance. I can't remember all the questions.... We have no reporters. You have three and are getting copies of the record and it isn't available to us. We haven't objected to this, but I think you should let* [Maple] *answer the questions and give him time to explain. If you slow down, I will try in my slow way to take it down.*[91]

Biddle added that he didn't know shorthand and couldn't write very fast but would take it down in his own "feeble way." To this complaint the prosecutor asserted it was the first time in his life he had ever heard such a request, followed with a long explanation of his duties in cross-examining witnesses and finally saying no, he wasn't going to slow down for the defense to take notes. A little kerfuffle ensued regarding Maple reading his own typed statement from the witness stand. A prosecution lawyer argued it shouldn't be called a statement. "I don't care what you call it; the mere fact that he reads something off a paper doesn't make it a statement. He is testifying as a witness, and this is merely his testimony and it is no statement. It is nothing to be attached to any record because it goes into the record every time he opens his mouth. This is merely his giving testimony."[92]

In addition to reading his statement during his testimony, Maple actively participated in the trial by personally cross-examining most of the prosecution witnesses against him. He corrected one lawyer by pointing out magna cum laude meant "with high praise," not, as the counselor said, "with the highest praise." During the prosecutor's questioning of a witness named Paul Kissman, the prosecutor was abruptly corrected by Maple. The prosecutor had asked Kissman about shirts that Kissman acknowledged purchasing in Denver; Maple interrupted to point out that Kissman had testified to buying only one shirt. On this minor point of clarification the prosecutor exclaimed, "By jove, you've got me again."[93]

The trial was off-limits to the public, but after the sentence was announced, the major general stated he wanted the results given wide publicity to dissuade others, both military and civilian, who might be tempted to give aid or comfort to enemy prisoners. Including the word "enemy" before "prisoners" (aren't all prisoners the enemy?) might have stemmed from an abundance of caution because the defense argued (unsuccessfully) that since the prisoners were safely detained in an enclosed camp in the United States, thousands of miles from the battlefields, they should no longer be characterized as the enemy. Maple claimed he was only detaining, not aiding, the two prisoners when he drove them to Mexico.

For a definition of "enemy," the court cited several examples and reached back to the Civil War to reference Congressman Benjamin G. Harris of Maryland, who was found guilty in a court-martial for harboring (providing a night's lodging) and giving money (one dollar each) to two paroled Confederate soldiers. For this, Harris got three years' imprisonment and was disqualified from ever holding any office of the United States, a sentence subsequently remitted by President Andrew Johnson. According to the Judge Advocate's Opinion, the Court Martial Manual of 1921 defined enemy as "enemy citizens as well as soldiers and does not restrict itself to the enemy government or its army. All the citizens of one belligerent are enemies of the government and of all the citizens of the other."[94]

## ARTICLE 81

The Judge Advocate General's Office informed *New Yorker* writer E.J. Kahn that in addition to the four defendants in the Maple case (Maple and the three privates who assisted him in his attempted escape: Paul Kissman, Theophil Leonhard and Frederich Siering), there were only four other convictions of Article 81 during World War II. As a side note, there was only one approved conviction of Article 81 in World War I, that of a private telling the enemy that he and his fellow soldiers would desert to the German army on reaching the front and would fight for the enemy. He was sentenced to twenty years confinement.[95]

Two of the four World War II cases related to assisting German prisoners' escapes by furnishing supplies and information about the location of German agents in Mexico, a revolver, compass and clothing. One case dealt with Max Stephan, a Detroit tavern keeper, who got a five-year sentence for harboring Hans Krug, a prison escapee from a camp in Ontario, Canada. Stephan furnished Krug with money and clothes and provided the name of a woman in Chicago who would help him get back to Germany. Krug got picked up by authorities before he could leave Chicago and later testified against Stephan. Stephan was sentenced to hang by the neck until dead. The Supreme Court refused to intervene, but President Roosevelt commuted the sentence in July 1943 just a few hours before it was to be enacted, pointing out that Stephan's actions were not premeditated.[96]

In October 1944, an American Air Corps lieutenant named Martin Monti flew a plane from an American airbase in Italy to Germany, where he spent several months working and communicating with the Nazis, even making radio broadcasts under the pseudonym Martin Wiethaupt. Upon his return, he claimed the plane had been shot down and that he had been taken prisoner until he eventually escaped. He was charged with desertion and illegally taking the plane but was found guilty of just taking the plane. His fifteen-year sentence was commuted in 1946 to time already served.[97]

Private Dale S. Lipps, from Harrison County, West Virginia, was found guilty in 1944 of Article of War 81 for giving a compass to a prisoner, and of Article 96 for fraternizing, consorting with and counseling nine prisoners near Bizerte, Tunisia, by giving them a bottle of aspirin tablets, lice powder, *Stars and Stripes* newspapers, a small bottle of iodine, cigarettes, playing cards, a can of black pepper and a dollar each in

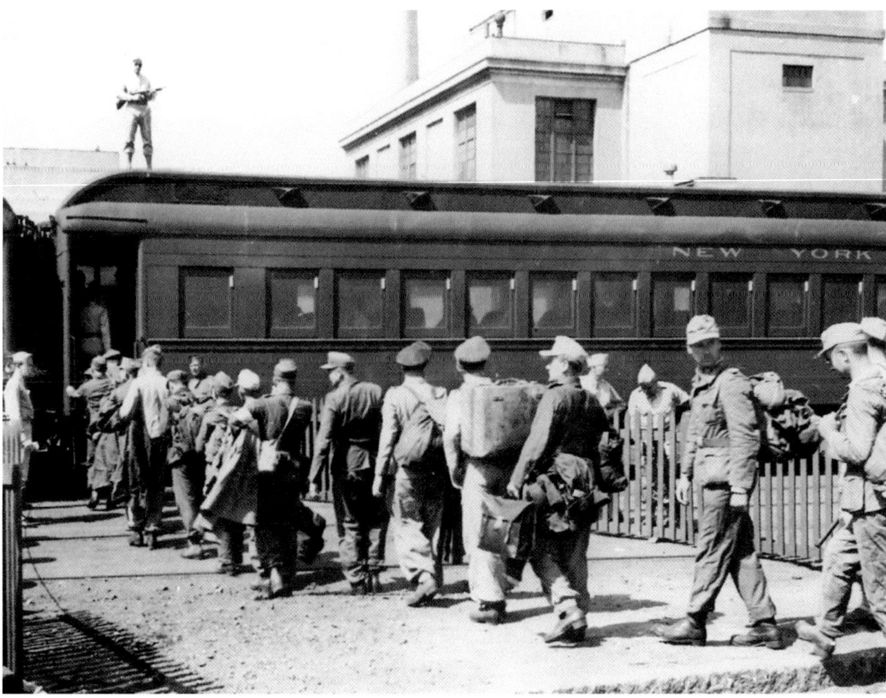


Prisoners being transferred to camps. *Courtesy of National Archives.*

American currency. And on at least one occasion, Lipps took a prisoner to the hospital to listen to a news broadcast. Private Lipps was sentenced to execution by hanging, but the sentence was subsequently reduced to ten years confinement.[98]

# 5

# The Best They Could with What They Had

At Maple's court-martial trial, the prisoners who had attempted to escape with him testified through interpreters. The acting judge advocate ruled the "so help me God" part of the oath should be omitted if the prisoners requested the omission. Pursuant to the Geneva Convention the prisoners could not be tried by court-martial and shouldn't be penalized for trying to escape; in fact, they had a duty to try. The prisoners were advised they didn't have to answer incriminating or degrading questions, but the transcript reads as if they weren't required to answer any questions at all. The deferential questioning indicates any information obtained from them must have been considered a bonus to the prosecution.

The laconic Kikillus, thirty-three, a "stabswachtmeister" (master sergeant) in the Afrika Korps, didn't say much more than his name. No one pressed him. Erhard Schwichtenberg, twenty-four, an "unteroffizier" (corporal), talked extensively but didn't say much more than what was already known. Schwichtenberg said he had been in the German army for five years, serving in the Afrika Korps until his capture in Carbona in May 1943 and shipment to the United States two months later. Before the war, he worked in a laboratory in the milk industry. He had provided the Eduard Müeller identification papers to Maple. He didn't know the trio had made it into Mexico until after they were apprehended. With Kikillus he planned to return to Germany but didn't know where Maple intended to go had the escape been successful. Schwichtenberg stated that when apprehended he was wearing his prisoner clothes with the letters "PW" removed or covered

POWs working on an ambulance. *Courtesy of the Mississippi Armed Forces Museum–Birdsong Collection.*

by his jacket. He refused to answer any questions about how he escaped from the prison camp.

As for his earlier New Year's Eve soiree in Denver, Schwichtenberg testified that he did not have authority to leave camp. He refused to answer a question about how he was dressed for the holiday weekend. (What an enemy soldier wears is no trivial matter; it is an important factor in deciding whether to press espionage charges.)[99]

The defense argued Maple had no malicious intent—that is, he escaped because he thought it unfair to be assigned to a camp of disloyal soldiers, and furthermore, it was un-American that such a camp existed. Maple's motivation, the defense argued, was to attract publicity, nothing more. That publicity would lead to the terminations of the camps. The soldiers of the 620th would be integrated back into regular army ranks again and not be subject to ostracism and contempt for being relegated to special organizations. That, according to the defense, is what motivated Maple. Helping Nazi prisoners escape from their stockade was just another means to achieve that end.

But Maple and his defense team knew the evidence of Maple having talked about setting off explosives throughout the United States couldn't be dismissed as the idle chatter of a misguided young man. After all, Maple had admitted to planning violence and sabotage to Agent Bryce in his own typed statement, which was made on his free will and accord, without any threats or promises and with the knowledge that it could be used against him later in court. Maple tried to defuse this by saying that some of his own statements to Bryce were inaccurate; they weren't lies because he claimed he had begun the interview with Agent Bryce by saying that many of his answers would be false. Bryce was not asked at trial whether Maple had warned him that some answers would be false. Maple's statement, which Maple personally typed, didn't mention anything about knowingly providing false, misleading or inaccurate information.

Maple claimed different things at different points. He suggested his discussions with his fellow members of the 620th concerning acts of sabotage and violence were not genuine but rather were part of a sting operation—that is, Maple claimed he was compiling and gathering information against his comrades to later turn over to authorities. Providing this evidence, Maple asserted, would help him prove his loyalty to America. To learn the plotters' plans, he claimed, he had to first gain their trust; hence, it was all a ruse, from the German accent to the German heritage to the fervent Nazi beliefs.

He said acts don't indicate intent, making the point with a Latin expression. Shoehorning Latin in at the trial seemed pedantic, a line more suited for debate team than a court-martial trial. Certainly the court knew Maple's intellectual gifts included a command of twenty-some languages. Just as odd, Maple also told the court he graduated high school at age fifteen, first in a class of some 1,500, but the correct figures were actually sixteen and 585. Maple needed others to know he was the smartest one in the room.

At Harvard, Maple said one of his professors was particularly influential. He had become active in the college German Club, serving as its treasurer. All the outrageous conduct and comments were part of a scheme to give the German Government confidence that Maple shared their beliefs. He naïvely thought "this storm of publicity would die a natural death if left by itself" and that his name would soon be forgotten. He stated that, at the time of the press coverage for his ROTC dismissal in late 1940, before Pearl Harbor, public opinion polls in America showed it was no more un-American to be pro-German than pro-British, and that World War II was not America's war. His father urged him to deny all the statements attributed to him. Maple said he didn't realize the wisdom of his father's advice until later. He admitted calling the German embassy the day after Pearl Harbor, as a "desperate act, an act of hysteria," a last-ditch effort to get to Germany. He conspicuously left out of his court testimony, however, something he had included in his typed statement: The purpose of the telephone call was to offer to join the German army and make his services available to them.

After graduating from Harvard, he returned to pursue a graduate degree. On the side, he obtained employment on a research project under the auspices of the U.S. Government. But two weeks later, word came from Washington terminating his involvement in the project. America didn't want him because of his pro-Hitler and pro-German beliefs; Germany didn't want him because he was too notorious and infamous to be useful. He was lost between countries.

> *I was then left in the position of being in a country at war with the country whose ideals I wished to uphold....My attitude toward the United States had always been not that I wished to see her defeated, or her form of government changed, but simply that Germany must not be destroyed. I felt that any part I might have had in destroying Germany by joining the Army would more than be offset by the influence I might be able to exert in peace-time, once my attitude toward this country had been established as not hostile.*[100]

Maple concluded he needed to join the U.S. armed forces to prove his patriotism. "I must become a member of the armed forces. In no better way could I better rid my name of the disrepute which it had acquired. Here was an emergency for which I had trained seven years in the ROTC. Here was a challenge to America from which I could not hide even in a university. In two months the first semester's work would be finished. So long I would wait, but no longer."[101]

So he joined the U.S. Army. In the army, he was closely monitored and his mail censored. Maple claimed he welcomed the scrutiny, believing it would eventually clear his reputation. Once again, however, the statement Maple read at his court-martial differed from the written statement he had given Agent Bryce. The court heard Maple's frustration about being assigned to a camp of disloyal soldiers and his claim that his actions resulted from his resentment. But it didn't hear the part about Maple characterizing himself as a determined Nazi ready to work with members of the special organizations to commit sabotage and other subversive actions.

Another important omission was that Maple wrote in his statement that he knew the two prisoners he took with him to Mexico were legal enemies of the United States, a fact he omitted from trial testimony.

The original plan had Private Leonhard going on furlough to Mexico in advance, to scout things out and prepare for Maple and Private Siering. They would leave on a Friday night, hoping their absence wouldn't be noticed until the following Monday morning. But the departure scheduling didn't work. The plan fizzled out because Leonhard couldn't get a furlough, Siering got cold feet, and matters in Argentina had "become somewhat uncertain." No further explanation was provided about Argentina; the inference being that some combination of Maple, Leonhard and Siering intended to end up there. The plan morphed temporarily into Maple going alone and borrowing Siering's car. But Siering, who couldn't agree to such usufruct, didn't want his car used in the plot unless he was driving it, which wasn't practicable for never-specified personal reasons. When Maple got wind of a rumor that the 620th was about to be transferred to Omaha, he decided to leave immediately rather than wait for a Friday.

No matter how hard he tried, Maple testified, he couldn't get authorities to stop and detain him. The police were "unobligingly unobservant. No one noticed our noisy presence." He drove the car into a ditch, on the opposite side of the road no less, and all he got was assistance from another motorist. He drove on a flat tire, with "the rattle of the steel rim on the concrete road" and headlights turned off at night and still couldn't draw the desired suspicion, partly he later learned, because of the delay at the camp in anyone noticing the prisoners' absence.

> *I had no choice but to go further. If my plans were to succeed, it was necessary that the escape appear genuine—that my actions be considered and publicized as treason. If I should go to the police station to surrender myself and the prisoners, such publicity would not be achieved. My voluntary surrender would seem incompatible with an act of treason. I would immediately be returned to the Army.…Only my seemingly involuntary apprehension would give my conduct the necessary note of authenticity. This difficulty plagued me henceforth. On the one hand, I could not turn myself in; and on the other, I could not continue on indefinitely.…If I followed the main highways and passed through the large towns, the car would be recognized and my problem would be solved. The car was a 1934 Reo and was almost unique. The police would have no difficulty identifying the car without regard even to the license plates. I proceeded southward*

Quonset house barracks. *Courtesy of Don James.*

*in confidence, not suspecting that the absence of the prisoners would go unnoticed for another 24 hours.*[102]

By the time the trio made it to the border, it looked like they had the unlucky misfortune of being unnoticed, even as they crossed into Mexico. Maple worried that he'd find himself in Berlin if such misfortune continued. He claimed that if he and the prisoners had made it fifty miles into Mexico they would have then turned back and given themselves up. But since they were apprehended just two or three miles over the Mexican border, they didn't get the chance.

## STATEMENTS OF COCONSPIRATORS

Eric Hotelling didn't testify at Maple's court-martial, but he admitted everything to army investigators, including the sabotage and mutiny plots. He claimed the plans represented a defensive measure only to protect himself, his friends in the 620th and the United States. The army didn't court-martial Hotelling, writing him off as a "damn-fool, crack-pot, and liar…entirely devoid of any practical sense." An army investigator opined that Hotelling was an "unquestionably sane and deadly serious" egotist who would "become a second Tito" if given the slightest opportunity. "Highly intelligent in an academic sense," Hotelling and his compatriots might have been smart enough to take over Camp Hale and release the prisoners of war, but "they were too dumb to understand that the plan was to be placed in effect only in the event of a communistic revolution, in which event many privates of the 620th Engineers would become colonels by grace of Hotelling's superior planning. There is no evidence that anyone took him seriously."[103]

Frederick Maurer said he suspected Maple planned to escape with two or three prisoners of war. Additionally Maurer admitted buying the .38 Colt revolver under a fictitious name and giving it to Paul Kissman, who gave it to Maple.[104]

Paul Kissman, born in Erie, Pennsylvania, to a German father and an American mother, had studied analytical chemistry in college, worked as a refrigeration inspector for General Electric and had traveled to Germany before his induction in the army in October 1941. Prior to his transfer to the 620th, Kissman worked in the medical corps. He had a brother serving in the transportation corps in the Pacific.

One of the trial's odd moments came when Paul Kissman was asked if he recognized anyone in the courtroom who had been on the sawmill detail the day Maple escaped, the idea being he would quickly identify and point to Maple, who was sitting at the defense table. But instead, like a gumshoe detective, according to E.J. Kahn in the *New Yorker*, Kissman "walked over to the court members and peered intently at every face, including the major general's. Then, having provoked mild tittering among those present, and having ostensibly assured himself that none of those Olympian gentlemen had been [Maple's] subordinates that day, he got down to business and said, 'Private Maple, sir. He is the only one around here.'"[105]

Kissman claimed he tried to dissuade Maple from escaping, believing Maple had little chance of success. Kissman had visited Germany from August 1939 to March 1940. On the question of what should happen to Maple if Maple were found guilty of aiding in the escape of two prisoners, Kissman stated he should get the death penalty. Maple later refused to testify at Kissman's court-martial but the army realized the folly of pressing contempt charges against Maple. Kissman was sentenced to life, which was shortened to twenty-five years by the court-reviewing authority.[106]

Theophil Leonhard, according to Eric Hotelling, was "the heart and soul" of the pro-Nazi movement in the 620th.[107] Leonard, along with Hugo Upton, had lived with Maple in a Deadwood house when the 620th was stationed in South Dakota. It was Leonhard's note about giving up his life that the prisoners were carrying when they were apprehended in Mexico. In the message, Leonhard wrote that he would continue to lead efforts to aid Germany: "And when you return to the native country, please dear friends, tell the authorities, especially the intelligence service about the things I mentioned....If the German agents will get in contact with me, everything will be possible." In interviews with the U.S. military, Leonhard claimed he didn't have any definite plans for espionage, sabotage or mutiny but was prepared to carry out instructions for subversive activity given him by German authorities.[108]

Leonhard told the army that he often heard Maple, as well as other members of the 620th, venting frustration and disgust with the army and talking about going over the hill, jargon for departing one's post or camp without approved leave.

## *Frederich Siering*

Frederich Wilhelm Siering told the court that Maple often talked about leaving camp and making his way to Germany, but Siering chalked it up to silly chatter and thought it was a joke. "Who," Siering asked from the witness stand, "wants to go to Germany in wartime?"

Although soldiers in the 620th had been restricted from owning cars, Siering obtained an unofficial exemption to keep his car because he and his wife lived with a pregnant woman. Perhaps the officer in charge just looked the other way and didn't enforce the prohibition against Siering. Maple, who knew Siering was the only member of the 620th with a car, sprang a surprise request on Siering on Saturday morning, February 12, 1944. Maple asked Siering to use his car to pick something up at Camp Hale. Siering agreed. What they picked up later that day turned out to be rucksacks that Maple and Private Leonhard had previously hidden at the Camp Hale dump. Siering and Maple loaded the rucksacks in the trunk of Siering's car. Siering kept them in his trunk as he drove back to his off-base residence. Later the next day, Maple and Paul Kissman drove to Siering's house in the Reo that Maple had just purchased. The rucksacks were then transferred from Siering's car to the Reo, and Siering agreed to let Maple park the Reo, with the rucksacks in it, in Siering's garage, located adjacent to the house Siering rented in Red Cliff, about five miles from Camp Hale.

Siering testified at Maple's court-martial and was also interviewed outside court several times by military investigators. Siering generally admitted to the facts. He originally said he knew Maple was going to attempt an escape to Germany, but at trial, he backpedaled, claiming he knew only that Maple was taking a three-day furlough and didn't know Maple was planning to take any prisoners with him.

But at Siering's court-martial trial in August 1945, more than a year after Maple's trial, Siering's defense counsel argued vociferously to keep Siering's earlier statements out of the trial. Siering's lawyers contended Siering hadn't been properly advised of his rights, didn't understand English very well, hadn't sworn to any statements and didn't have the opportunity to review the investigator's report. Siering was charged with Article of War 81 for helping load and conceal the rucksacks as well as for taking prisoner Schwichtenberg (with Private Leonhard) to Denver for the New Year's Eve trip. Siering refused to answer questions about how he was dressed on that holiday outing.

Siering stated he was subsequently asked on several other occasions by various prisoners of war to take them out of camp for a visit into town but refused those requests because of the regret he felt for having taken Schwichtenberg out over the New Year's weekend. He wasn't going to make that mistake a second time, or at least he wasn't going to get caught twice. The prosecutor's questions about Siering having two brothers in the German army and about Siering purportedly saying he would never fight against Germany were cut off by a defense objection, which was sustained.

Maple testified at Siering's court-martial and said he kept many details of the escape plan from Siering because he considered Siering unreliable. Maple added: "The situation of our company was rather odd. I might say we were all almost dubious about [Siering's] disloyalty. All the members of the company were under suspicion and we naturally rated one another as being more or less properly placed in that organization and we were never sure that Fritz [Siering] could be trusted."[109]

Siering's defense counsel argued that yes, Siering had taken a prisoner of war on the weekend trip to Denver but that he brought the prisoner back to camp, no harm had been done to the United States—"at least no great harm"—there were no acts of sabotage and there was no evidence to show the prisoner communicated with enemy forces during the trip.[110]

Another member of Siering's defense team took a cautious approach, saying upfront that his remarks were not intended to criticize the laws, the government, the congress or the armed forces but that, respectfully, the Denver holiday trip was simply about American soldiers proudly showing off America to a prisoner of war, boasting that any man in America could have a nice life, earn money and own a home.

A third defense attorney was neither cautious nor meek. Without nuance or apologies, Defense Counsel Gutting blasted the charges, accusing military intelligence of "scraping the bottom of the barrel in this prosecution… with mixed facts for confessions…[because] the big shots on up wanted to prosecute [Siering]."

Defense Counsel McNaughton claimed that "one hair on his [Siering's] head is worth more than all of Maple, Kissman or any of the other guys who are American citizens and who are sitting in the pen." He called the proceedings melodramatic, pointing out the army's bad judgment in placing a prisoner of war camp of some 250 inmates, mostly German soldiers, next to the 620th, which consisted mainly of German sympathizers. "It was bound to happen, those things that did happen." He implored the court to understand the critical significance of Maple saying he didn't trust Siering. This was the proof that Siering was not involved with Maple, under the enemy of my enemy is my friend theory: "This bird, could not be trusted with the secrets of the inner-council. Maple had clearly said he was intentionally evasive with Siering. What does that mean? You men are smart. Use your own judgment."

No evidence was presented to show Siering knew prisoners would be part of Maple's trip, regardless of whether the trip was an approved three-day furlough or an escape to Germany. Hence, Siering was found not guilty on the specifications and charges dealing with the rucksacks but was found guilty of Article of War 81 for his involvement in the New Year's Eve trip. It's unknown whether the court members knew of Siering's reputation in the 620th for communicating with the prisoners of war. Hotelling called Siering the "communicant."[111]

The court looked unfavorably on Siering's lies and deceptions regarding the holiday trip, registering at the hotel under a fictitious name, using army clothing to disguise the prisoner of war, letting the prisoner roam by himself in Denver and perhaps for lying to his wife about the prisoner's identity. Siering's wife also looked unfavorably on Siering. A few years later, by 1950, they were divorced, and Siering was reportedly living in Argentina.

Siering was dishonorably discharged and sentenced to ten years at hard labor, later reduced to five years at Fort Knox. Shortly after the sentencing, however, the army realized Siering had never been legally inducted into the army. Much like Private Loock, Siering, who was born in Germany, arrived illegally in New York City as an employee of the German merchant marine before the war. He walked off his ship onto land in 1936 and stayed in the United States, eventually making a home for himself and his wife in Chicago. His U.S. military service records

Camps held 435,000 POWs during World War II. *Courtesy of David Witte.*

reveal his character rating as excellent and his efficiency as a solider as satisfactory. The U.S. District Court ruled that Siering never renounced his German citizenship and was thus an alien enemy of the United States. He would have been deported except for the war. He was called up for service and sent to an induction center, where he refused to take the oath. His claims were ignored. Citing the *Billings v. Truesdell* case, the court ruled Siering was not subject to military rules and ordered the military to release him. Siering's sentence was vacated, and Siering was discharged on May 27, 1946.[112]

## Billings v. Truesdell

*To the "Harvardification" of this entire episode, from the perfidy of Maple to the brilliant literary summation by E.J. Kahn in the* New Yorker *and the indefatigable doggedness of the legal tactician and future congressman Charles O. Porter, comes the efforts of a Harvard alumnus named Arthur Goodwyn Billings, who successfully argued his own case before the nation's highest court. The case,* Billings v. Truesdell, *forced the U.S. military to revise its rules as to whom it could and could not court-martial. Truesdell was Captain Karl Truesdell Jr., who later became a major general in the army.*

*The* Harvard Crimson *reported in a story by Richard A. Burgheim in March 1952 that Billings, a former Harvard student with no legal training, "briefed, pleaded and won in the United States Supreme Court the only case the Army lost during* [World War II]." *The story stated Billings received his master's degree at Harvard in 1941 and, at that time (in March 1952), was preparing his doctorate thesis on the history of the Austrian economy. Billings had graduated with honors from the University of Kansas in 1933, worked for a few years in the American Diplomatic Service in Moscow and entered Harvard in the fall of 1938. As a conscientious objector during World War II, he was court-martialed by the army. He argued that since he never agreed to be inducted, he was never legally in the army. And since he was never in the army, the army had no right to punish–that is, court-martial–him. The case made its way to the U.S. Supreme Court, which had to decide whether someone could be legally inducted into the army against his will. If so, the military had the right to court-martial; if not, civilian courts had jurisdiction. The key, eight justices concluded against one opposed, was the oath and whether it was given voluntarily. The court ruled on March 27, 1944, that civilians become soldiers only when they swear an oath, not when they are accepted for duty after physical and mental examinations. If the oath wasn't legally obtained, there was no induction. This court ruling compelled the army to discharge many soldiers, including Fritz Loock, the man who disobeyed a direct order after getting advice from Maple.*

## Closing Remarks

Each of the three members of Maple's defense team made closing statements. Major Ohman, the non-lawyer counsel, claimed Maple didn't desert when he fled to Mexico. He was just trying to attract attention. If he had intended to escape he would have gone alone and not taken two "burdensome" prisoners of war with him. No, claimed Ohman, the case was about Maple's "strong mania to be in the public eye in a sensational way." In Maple, Ohman saw far more "egotism than tangible aid to Germany," which Ohman noted was six thousand miles from Camp Hale. Maple was "unbalanced and irresponsible," according to Ohman, and his problems stemmed from "unique and terrific" egotism, a "bloated opinion" of himself and a lack of "ordinary judgment and horse sense." Ohman suggested the court put little weight on the psychiatrists' conclusions because they had to form their opinions based solely on what Maple chose to tell them.[113]

At least six physicians—five of them psychiatrists—examined Maple in 1944.[114] One called him a "torch-bearer," another said he was "a very vicious type" and another concluded Maple believed what he was doing was right. All agreed he was sane. The prevailing theme among the psychiatrists dealt with the absurdity that Maple rationalized his acts with a complete lack of emotion. In various words, this "poverty of emotion" thread wove its way through most of the medical reports. Two of the conclusions found:

> [Maple] *to be normal and coherent in his speech, without delusions or paranoid trends, or hallucinations;* [with] *a normal orientation, unimpaired memory and a highly superior intelligence and intellectual development. Contrasted to these factors* [Maple showed] *a lack of concern over the outcome of the then impending court-martial trial, a poverty and superficiality of emotions, and an impaired insight and lack of mature judgment. There was no emotional warmth or development of lasting attachments, such as indicate criteria of adult behavior. Accused had not, however, lost any contact with reality, and even in one incident of "depersonalization" described to witness by accused, of the affectation of several Germanicisms for a time after he joined the 620th Engineers, accused's actions were conscious and purposeful. The impairment of insight and judgment was definitely not of psychotic proportions.*[115]

> [Maple] *does not appear to be sorry for himself. He knew the consequences of his act of treason and he planned the escape without any inspiration*

A sign as a weapon in World War II. *Courtesy of the Tenth Mountain Division Resource Center, Denver Public Library.*

> *from others. He is correctly oriented as to place, person, and date, shows no paranoid ideas, or depressive content. No delusional ideas were elicited. He certainly knows the difference between right and wrong and he is, in my opinion, legally responsible for his acts.*[116]

Lieutenant Fleischaker said in his closing comments that Maple had an "extraordinary academic mind," the most brilliant mind he had ever encountered, but one completely lacking common sense. "The more I saw him," Fleischaker said, "the more convinced I was of a genius and of an abnormal personality."[117]

Humphrey Biddle, the Kansas lawyer who had been defending soldiers in court-martial cases going back to World War I, said he had never seen a case like Maple's. He couldn't figure out Maple and added that Maple had not been much help to his attorneys. Biddle downplayed the charges by pointing out Maple didn't financially benefit and no one got hurt. "Foolish, of course," Biddle said, but "a killing did not result from this. No woman was insulted. There was really no sabotage, and I feel down in my own heart that he meant no harm to his country." Maple's actions, argued Biddle, were "so fantastic, so unusual, so unreal" that Maple couldn't be held responsible;

they must have been caused by a mental quirk. Maple needed treatment, not to "dangle at the end of a rope." Biddle claimed Maple was driven in large part in an attempt to draw attention to himself and to the existence of the army's special organizations.

Biddle suggested court members "look at this boy, if I may call him that" and imagine their reactions if their sons were on trial facing similar charges. "Decide this case under all the circumstances," Biddle implored, "as if he were your own flesh and blood." He believed Maple's defense was best summed up through Maple's father's testimony. "Naturally it was an appeal from a father to fathers, which undoubtedly many of you are."[118]

Maple also made a few closing remarks. He asked the court to "restore to me and my comrades the right to be American and the right to fight for our country. That is all that we have desired. That is all that I now desire, that we be allowed to participate in the defense and turn that defense to offense for our country."[119]

The prosecutor's summary statement did not go over the facts of the case. It consisted of acknowledging the work of the FBI, the military officers who handed the case to him "you might say, on a silver platter," and the defense team's "splendid manner" in "capably, fully, honestly and fairly" defending their client "the best they could with what they had." The prosecution agreed with the defense that the accused was entitled to the benefit of any reasonable doubt, emphasizing the point with a quote from the "immortal" Robert E. Lee: "Duty is the grandest word in the English language."[120]

Maple's problem, however, was Maple—that is, all his own actions and statements. He had admitted to Agent Bryce, with other FBI agents present, that he planned to enter a sabotage school in Hamburg, Germany, with hopes of using those malevolent skills in the United States; that he and his coterie of saboteurs planned to round up and spread about 150 men throughout the western states (he hadn't determined how many were needed for the eastern states) to foment destruction throughout America by disrupting and destroying communication and transportation lines.

These oral statements were augmented with a map that Maple marked during his interview with Agent Bryce, a map showing key locations, where explosives were to be set. Maple certainly couldn't deny or explain away the map, perhaps the most important trial exhibit. In addition, the court was shown notes that Maple wrote to Paul Kissman while both were imprisoned at Leavenworth—more evidence that couldn't be explained away:

> *Yes, I am mixed up with a bunch of Germans (a lot of Italians and Americans too) and I've helped more than two men escape. I haven't seen what the papers say, but I was picked up in Mexico with two Prisoners of War. Right now I think most of the gang in New York are working to get the right men elected when election comes around.*
>
> *Paul: Trial on April 17. Will use abused Americanism angle. Will reveal sabotage plans, etc. Pass word to others: We'll lay it on thick.*
>
> *They have me here because they think I know a lot about German activities in this country and they want to pump me. They know they can't prove anything and that's why they don't want to try me. I was over the hill four days and I can beat a charge of desertion. I can't tell you who the boss is, but you'll get acquainted in NY with a lot of the fellows.*[121]

Had there been no map or statements or notes, Maple would have been on firmer ground but by no means in the clear. The facts of the case, virtually all undisputed, as well as Maple's deceptions, convicted him. A War Department report concisely summed it up when it concluded:

> *It is apparent to the most casual observer as it must have been apparent to the members of the court that the sympathies of accused are and at all times have been with the German Reich…motivated not by any patriotic impulse on the part of the accused to straighten out the deficiencies in the Armed Services of the United States, but by a desire to reach the German Reich with information of value and accompanied by two loyal German Prisoners of War whose liberty he had affected.*[122]

Legally the army had to prove just the facts; it didn't have to prove intent or motive. But even if it did, overwhelming evidence proved Maple's intent and motives were to escape and to help prisoners of war escape. Buying the car and the supplies, coordinating an escape with prisoners, feigning car trouble to evade detection, impersonating another person upon apprehension replete with the German accent and the fabricated personal background—none of it happened by accident or coincidence or spontaneity. The army did note, however, the few extenuating factors working in the accused's behalf. The accused:

1. did not wait to be drafted but enlisted voluntarily;
2. served for more than a year "without a blemish" on his military record;

3. surrendered a noncommissioned officer's rating to secure combat service;
4. served as an instructor in two camps prior to his transfer to the $620^{th}$;
5. was not informed why he was sent to a subversive unit or the purpose of the existence of such units.

In the end, those points didn't mean much. There was no denying that Maple did precisely what the charges claimed he did. The only question was whether he would be sentenced for life or executed. Was this a zealous traitor or a deeply misguided young man? The court decided the former. Dale Maple was found guilty in Court-Martial 257165 on May 8, 1944, and was sentenced to execution by hanging.

## The Destruction of Tyranny

Shortly after the trial, Major General Myron C. Cramer, the judge advocate general, recommended Maple's sentence be reduced to hard labor for life at Leavenworth and forfeiture of all pay and allowances:

> *There is no question of his sanity. Accused's acts were despicable and there appears little in the record other than accused's youth to suggest mitigation. I believe, however, that under all the circumstances justice does not require this young man's life and that the ends of justice will better be served by sparing his life so that he may live to see the destruction of tyranny, the triumph of the ideals against which he sought to align himself, and the final victory of that freedom he so grossly abused.*[123]

## Trial Critique

After the trial, the War Department reviewed the case and concluded the prosecution often improperly led witnesses but excused the leading questions as justified because many witnesses were hostile and evasive. The War Department also stated it was improper for the prosecution to have introduced the psychiatrists' findings and conclusions on an individual basis rather than as one item, followed by the opportunity to examine and cross-examine each witness. In addition, the War Department noted that the trial judge advocate failed to inquire whether Maple could distinguish right from wrong and adhere to the right. But the report concluded the presumption was in favor of sanity. In the absence of evidence to the contrary, the report concluded, there were no irregularities or errors that prejudiced Maple's rights.[124]

According to a report published by the U.S. House of Representatives in June 1946, there were 63,876 general court-martials in the United States during World War II, resulting in 60,110 convictions and 3,766 acquittals, an acquittal rate of 5.89 percent. The report surveyed the difficult terrain for defendants and their counsel:

> *When the court-martial authority appoints counsel not selected by the accused, the selection seems often to be unfortunate, so far as competent defense is concerned. Very young and inexperienced officers, or officers not very capable anyway who can readily be spared from other duties, or officers who whatever their responsibilities as counsel, of officers who fear bringing the ill will of higher authorities upon themselves by too energetic a defense—all these types appear in the story of court-martial cases. At best a defense counsel labors under disadvantages. He is often appointed a very short time before the trial and does not have opportunity to get a more thorough understanding of the case, whereas his adversary is usually more fully informed, and has, moreover, the backing of the judge advocate at headquarters. Defense counsel can secure the attendance of distant witnesses only by the aid and with the permission of the prosecution. Witnesses for the defense can be interfered with by the authorities by threats or promises, and sometimes are, while counsel for the defense has no power to resort to such practices even if he wanted to do so. Energetic defense counsel have been told they are obstructing justice, and sometimes wonder afterward why their expected promotions fail to come through.*[125]

## SILLY ROMANCE

Five women, members of the Women's Army Corps (WAC), got caught up in the wretched saga, fraternizing with prisoners, exchanging notes and presents and, on at least one occasion, meeting outside the barracks with a prisoner dressed as an American soldier. Few details, salacious or otherwise, were mentioned in the newspaper stories or army reports about how closely they fraternized or how the WACs assisted the prisoners. The WACs involved were in regular contact with prisoners on work details. The WAC mentioned most often in news accounts, Florence Pechon, passed notes between one of the prisoners (Schwichtenberg) and Maple, believing they were cousins. Schwichtenberg kept a love letter from one of the WACs in his prison barracks and boasted that certain WACs offered to bring the prisoners anything they wanted. Pechon's mother chalked the ruckus up to the fact that her daughter was "just a big, good-natured, red-headed girl who would set any camp in an uproar."

The *Troy Record* characterized the ignominy as an "indiscretion," and a report by the judge advocate general (JAG) called it a "silly romance" on the part of the WACs. Whatever it was, the army press release stated the WACs had nothing to do with the two prisoners who escaped with Maple. The actions of the WACs could not be condoned, but according to the JAG report, they shouldn't be charged with Article of War 81 because they hadn't been given sufficient orders and instructions explaining the rules against fraternizing. Instead, they pleaded guilty to violation of Article of War 96 and were sentenced to six months' confinement at hard labor at the WAC Guardhouse in Des Moines and forfeiture of two-thirds of their pay. Article 96 did not mention fraternizing with the enemy or anything at all about the enemy. It concerned conduct bringing discredit upon the military.

Once the sentences had been served, the army concluded, there would not be a recurrence of these offenses because "these girls" would be reassigned to new stations and separated from each other. Presumably they would also be separated in the future from prisoners.[126]

6

# Leavenworth

Four years after Maple's court-martial, Charles Orlando Porter entered the case. According to one of Porter's letters to E.J. Kahn, Porter had known Maple at Harvard, and on at least one occasion, they had gone on a double date with Wellesley students.[127] After college, Porter joined the army,

Soldiers in the 620th were directed to sell their cars or put them in storage. *Courtesy of David Witte.*

and by the spring of 1945, he was working on war crimes in the European Theater of Operations.

Porter encountered immediate obstacles from the Leavenworth warden, who said there was no record of Porter being Maple's attorney. The warden, Walter A. Hunter, claimed he checked with Maple, and Maple said no, Porter wasn't his attorney and, furthermore, that Maple had no legal work for Porter or any other lawyer. Warden Hunter had intercepted and read Porter's letters to Maple and was convinced Porter was trying to publicize the case. Such actions were, the warden noted, "definitely against the policy of the Bureau of Prisons. Under the circumstances it is not possible to grant your request for a visit." At the same time, Maple's mother was complaining to Porter that the "fussy" warden was reviewing and delaying Maple's outgoing letters from Fort Leavenworth.[128]

## Your Boy's Battered Head

The warden correctly suspected Porter was trying to generate publicity. Porter's efforts to drum up attention started in September 1948 with a letter to E.J. Kahn, who at the time was periodically writing stories for the *New Yorker*.

"Because I think you could do a good job of it," Porter wrote to Kahn, "I'm offering you a chance to write an article about the only American soldier ever convicted of treason." Porter pointed out that it was a complex case because the prisoner was a genius—that is, he "scored within a certain range on standard intelligence tests"—but was "stupid, however, in some respects." Porter intentionally omitted Maple's name in his initial contact with Kahn because Porter didn't want someone else "muscling in on what is a first rate story." Kahn immediately took interest and began research. Kahn interviewed several of Maple's former classmates, including James Hawkes—described by Porter as "the big wheel in the German Club"—professors, fellow ROTC members, Maple's commanding officer from Fort Bragg, a major in the army reserve who was "disgustingly terrified lest his name be dragged in and the army be displeased" and a few soldiers who had been at Camp Hale with Maple. Porter provided Kahn with a copy of the voluminous court-martial files, which Porter had received from Maple's mother.

To devise a strategy, Porter and Kahn organized a "bull-session" with several of Maple's former friends and associates, including an MIT assistant professor and a Harvard economics PhD candidate. Kahn wanted information for a

Camp Concordia barracks.
*Courtesy of Audrey Kalivoda.*

magazine article, and Porter hoped a piece in the coveted *New Yorker* might help Maple get released early from Leavenworth. Porter advised Kahn that his intention was to get Maple out of jail, "not indict the army."[129]

Porter stated he had invited a professor from the Harvard Philology Department to the bull-session but was told the philology professors disliked Maple and didn't want to cooperate. Afterward, both writer and lawyer thought the meeting had been helpful. Porter said, "The soiree was fascinating." Kahn agreed it was worthwhile as well as fascinating.

Kahn also interviewed Maple's mother, Mrs. Scoville, in Newport. Kahn concluded she had been badly misinformed in thinking the 620th was made up "by and large, of nice, misunderstood boys." Her remarks to Kahn, no matter how well intended to help Maple's case, apparently weren't convincing. "I'm sorry to have to say that some of the stuff I did learn," Kahn wrote to Porter, "doesn't exactly put a halo on your boy's battered head."[130]

Porter acknowledged the evidence against Maple in the court-martial trial was difficult to rebut, especially Maple's prison notes to Kissman: "Abused American angle. Ow. We'll lay it on thick. Ow twice."[131]

By July 1949, Kahn heard comments that *Collier's* was planning a magazine story about Maple but suspected it might be just a rumor designed to make Kahn nervous. Nothing came of this, and there is no indication *Collier's* ever published a detailed story about Maple. Kahn ended up getting his story published in 1950 in the *New Yorker*, in a masterful series entitled "The Philologist," broken up into four parts: "A Trip to Old Palomas," "Dissonance in the Tower," "A State of Agitation" and "Who Wants to Go to Germany in Wartime?"[132]

## Life in Prison

In prison, Maple kept busy, playing basketball, dominoes, handball and shuffleboard, and he boxed, at one point breaking two ribs in the process. He worked on improving his foreign languages, especially Japanese, French and Spanish. He wrote occasional pieces for the quarterly prison publication, *The New Era*, including an article about overlapping and conflicting regulations between the states and the federal government, specifically complaining that a state could charge a person after he was released from federal prison.

He taught several subjects at Leavenworth, including trigonometry. He read vociferously, brushed up on his shorthand and played bridge, admitting in a letter that one of his fellow inmates was a better bridge player. Although Maple had much free time, he still felt rushed. He wrote letters, including one to ask his mother to make a five-dollar donation in his name to the Harvard Glee Club for an upcoming overseas trip. He still owed money to Harvard in 1947. He couldn't make it to the sixth reunion of the class of 1941; the reunion report simply stated he did not return the questionnaire. In 1947, three years into his prison term and ten years after his high school graduation, he learned San Diego High School had bestowed on him an award for academic excellence.

In prison, Maple was allowed to receive seven letters a week, of which he allotted three for his mother. He could spend up to ten dollars per month in the prison commissary. As of December 1944, his first Christmas in prison, he was allowed to receive one package weighing no more than two pounds.

Major General Cramer's recommendation to reduce Maple's sentence to life in prison made its way up the chain, through Secretary of War Henry Stimson to General Edwin Watson at the White House and eventually to President Roosevelt, who approved it on November 18, 1944. On hearing the news, Maple wrote that it was a bit of a shock. He added he might spend a long time in prison and live to 108.[133] In March 1946, the sentence was reduced again, this time to ten years' imprisonment. In the end, Maple was released on October 8, 1950, about seven months after Kahn's *New Yorker* articles. Whether Porter and Kahn's efforts resulted in or hastened Maple's release is unknown and speculative. By that point, U.S. soldiers were fighting another war in Korea. In total, Maple served about six and a half years in prison. Toward the end, Maple wrote letters to the warden arguing that his release date should be moved up twenty-nine days based on Maple's determination that he was entitled to more days than the authorities had calculated for statutory good time.

# Epilogue

Maple said deceiving his parents about the money he borrowed from them, ostensibly to pay Harvard but really to fund the car and the escape, was "the only painful episode in the whole affair" and that his only regret was not spending more time with his music.[134]

After prison, he returned to San Diego and eventually got into the maritime insurance business. In the early 1980s, he was mentioned in a lawsuit as a representative of the American National General Insurance Agencies. The case, relating to damage to barges along the Delaware River, made its way in 1984 to the U.S. Court of Appeals for the Third Circuit.[135] He died on May 28, 2001, in the San Diego suburb of El Cajón.

Dale Maple's father, L.G. Maple, got into a bit of legal trouble later in life. The *San Bernardino County Sun* of July 9, 1961, carried a photograph of him, identified as a construction superintendent of the U.S. National Bank, a bank owned by a Conrad Arnholt Smith. Smith's bank topped off with sixty-two branches and almost $1 billion in assets before going bankrupt and being taken over by the FDIC in 1973, in what was reported at the time as the largest bankruptcy in U.S. history. The *Bakersfield Californian* of January 20, 1974, reported that L.G. Maple, vice-president of the bank, signed a phony $600,000 note, and the *San Bernardino County Sun* reported on September 3, 1976, that he signed a $750,000 promissory note as an officer for Kingsburg Oil Company, an entity of which he later claimed no knowledge. Other employees also admitted signing fraudulent notes as officers for fictitious companies. Smith, otherwise known as "Mr. San Diego" for his penchant for making big business deals, was convicted in 1979 of tax fraud and embezzling $8.9 million.

JELLYBEAN BRYCE RETIRED FROM the FBI in 1958. Upon retirement, he was a GS-15 earning $12,420 per year. Shortly after retirement, he ran for governor of Oklahoma, as an Independent. The hot issues of the day were legalizing liquor and hunting down Communists. He was against the former and for the latter. He claimed he knew of every Communist in the state and that he'd make sure none of them would ever hold office in Oklahoma. A memo in Bryce's personnel file indicates that Bryce was allegedly telling people that one of his gubernatorial opponents was a Communist and that the FBI had a "fat file" about him. Despite great slogans like "Vote your convictions" and "Get out of a jam with Jelly," the flamboyant maverick went down to overwhelming defeat.

In April 1944, Hoover commended Bryce for his work in apprehending a fugitive in Mexico. Two months earlier, Bryce had interviewed Dale

"Think and vote Independent." *Courtesy of the Oklahoma Publishing Company Collection at the Oklahoma Historical Society.*

Maple after Maple was apprehended in Mexico. But there aren't any letters in Bryce's file about Maple. In fact, there is only a single mention of Maple in Bryce's entire personnel file, and it deals with someone named Martin O'Neill writing a letter on *Time* magazine stationery in August 1975 to the director of the FBI. In the letter, O'Neill requested information about Bryce for an upcoming movie about Maple, tentatively called *The Little Known Soldier*. The FBI didn't appear interested in cooperating.

Showing the form that got Jelly Bryce into *Life* magazine. *Courtesy of Ron Owens.*

Five years after retiring from the FBI, Bryce filed a worker's compensation claim for hearing loss due to the noise from gunfire. He was awarded $1,914.17 as compensation. He died of a heart attack in May 1974 while attending a reunion of former FBI special agents.

IN THE DECADES FOLLOWING the war, many former prisoners returned as tourists to the United States to visit what remained of the camps and places where they had been detained and, in many cases, to visit with fellow prisoners and Americans who had worked at the camps. Nine of the three thousand Germans who had been imprisoned during the war at Camp Trinidad returned two decades later. The City of Trinidad invited the former wartime prisoners for the reunion. The former prisoners were met at Stapleton Field by a contingent of Trinidad residents headed by a former mayor and by the director of state institutions, who greeted the group on behalf of the governor, who was out of the city. The city manager said several activities were planned in Trinidad for the visitors.[136]

E.J. KAHN RECEIVED WELL-DESERVED commendations for his story. Nathaniel Weyl, who had just published a book about treason in 1950, wrote to Kahn saying he was slightly embarrassed because the facts he used in his brief account of the Maple affair came from Pentagon officials "who garbled the facts."[137]

Charles Orlando Porter served as a member of the United States House of Representatives, from Oregon in the Eighty-Fifth and Eighty-Sixth Congresses, from January 1957 to January 1961. He was defeated in his 1960 reelection bid.

Arthur G. Billings assisted in the 1940 presidential election of Norman Thomas, the Socialist candidate. The *Harvard Crimson* reported in its November 5, 1940 issue that Billings had introduced Thomas on November 4, in what the *Crimson* reported was Thomas's last speech of the campaign. Billings got into politics himself a few years later when, in 1944, he ran as a Socialist from Kansas for a seat in the U.S. Senate.

Eric Hotelling stated that all charges against him were dropped because there wasn't "a shred of evidence."[138] He later obtained a master's and a doctorate with a 209-page dissertation, "Polycyclic Quaternary Ammonium Salts."[139] In 1954, he coauthored an article with the same title published in the *Journal of the American Chemical Society*. As vice-president for research and technology of Yoo-Hoo Chocolate Beverage Corporation, he testified in 1968 as a noted expert in food chemistry before the U.S. Senate. His biography boasted authorship or coauthorship of twelve publications in technical journals and that he was the recipient of around forty patents.[140]

After their apprehension in Mexico, Schwichtenberg and Kikillus were transferred to a prisoner of war camp in Worland, Wyoming, a good distance farther from the Mexican border than Camp Hale. That additional distance didn't deter Schwichtenberg, who tried again to escape in June 1945 with two other prisoners. The trio cut the stockade's barbed-wire fence and crawled under it, but they didn't make it to Mexico or anywhere close. They were apprehended less than three hours after escaping.[141]

On March 1, 1944, the 620th officially disbanded and was renamed Camp A of the 1800th Engineer Service Battalion. Eventually, the three special organizations were merged together at Camp Forrest in Bell Buckle, Tennessee, as the 1800th ESB, with the former 620th becoming Company A, the 525th as Company B and the 358th as Company C.

Members of the special organizations complained to Congress and the president about their treatment. A private named Lorence Asman wrote a

American soldiers, foreign prisoners and Women Army Corps members were stationed at Camp Hale. *Courtesy of David Witte.*

fifteen-page letter to FDR calling the special organization to which he was assigned a concentration camp, urging someone to investigate how the army

> *dumped all of us into a big pot and let us stew in our own bitter juices.... An outfit like this should not exist....It is hard convincing people we are not prisoners of war. Our men have been attacked with knives and clubs by people who thought that very thing. It is not good to put men in the uniforms of the U.S. Army who should not be wearing it. There are some of us who have volunteered for overseas service and were anxious to help end the war.*

The audacious Senator Reynolds, with an unidentified constituent. *From Wikimedia Commons.*

> *But instead we were put into an organization like this to live like slaves and prisoners and criminals. Here we have university students, lawyers, doctors, musicians, writers and artists digging ditches and building roads.*[142]

Another letter claimed one of the officers hit one of the men over the head with a flashlight on New Year's Eve and threatened to shoot another at the firing squad. In December 1945, orders went out that no one in the 1800th could reenlist without specific approval.

Senator Robert Rice Reynolds of North Carolina, sometimes known as "Buncombe Bob" or "Showman Bob," followed up with an intensive investigation that included testimony from seventy-seven witnesses and more than six hundred pages. Reynolds was often criticized as loud and abrasive. In October 1941, at age fifty-seven, he married his fifth wife, a twenty-year-old society heiress. He served in the U.S. Senate from March 1933 until January 1945. He did not seek reelection in 1944.[143]

JOHN EDGAR HOOVER REPORTED that for fiscal year ending June 30, 1944, 13 people were indicted by federal grand juries for treason, including 8 for broadcasting propaganda via shortwave radio from Germany and Italy. There were 11 convictions in federal courts for violations of espionage statutes and 51 for sabotage laws, although Hoover noted there were 1,136 instances in which some form of sabotage, "mostly technical in nature," was uncovered. During the fiscal year, 54 individuals were convicted for harboring deserters and 14,695 federal fugitives had been rounded up, of which 8 were tried and convicted in federal courts. From the beginning of the war until June 30, 1944, 15,764 alien enemies were apprehended, consisting of 6,822

Germans, 5,353 Japanese, 3,565 Italians, 12 Hungarians, 11 Romanians and 1 Bulgarian. For fiscal year 1945, the FBI claimed 10 convictions in federal courts for espionage, 45 for sabotage, and an estimated 500 new sedition cases, of which approximately 200 had been declined for prosecution and 300 were pending.[144] As of November 1945, the army held approximately 33,700 prisoners in the United States spread among disciplinary barracks, rehabilitation centers and federal prisons.[145]

After the war, the United States fell short of fulfilling Article 75 of the Geneva Convention, which required prisoners be released with minimum delay and in any event as soon as the circumstances justifying their detention and internment ceased to exist. Many members of Congress pushed to quickly return the prisoners of war to Europe so that returning American soldiers would have jobs. But agricultural interests in the United States pushed harder for a delay. The labor shortage did not immediately end when the war did. Great efforts and labor had to be expended by Americans just to get the American soldiers back home. The war ended in August 1945, but President Truman granted an extension to return many of the prisoners until February 1946. With even more political pressure exerted, he granted an additional sixty days after that to alleviate the labor shortage, especially in work related to sugar beets, cotton and the pulpwood industry.

When the prisoners left the United States, they were allowed to take with them one bag weighing no more than thirty pounds. About 200,000 prisoners were sent back home to Germany or Austria in 1946 and 1947. To their surprise, however, many did not go back home but went instead to other European countries—primarily France, Great Britain, Belgium, Holland and Luxembourg—to work on farms, in coal mines and with general cleanup.[146]

The United States transferred 40,000 prisoners to Belgium, 10,000 to Holland and 7,000 to Luxembourg. At least 150,000 held in the United States were "British owned," and Great Britain wanted at least 130,000 of them after the war. Altogether, about 178,000 prisoners who had been held in the United States spent at least one year in French or British labor camps after the war. On July 23, 1946, the last 1,388 regular prisoners left the United States. The only remaining prisoners were 141 serving criminal sentences, 134 being treated at hospitals or psychiatric wards and the 25 who had escaped and were still on the loose.[147] A lieutenant colonel remarked after the war that the army wasn't in the prison business and that it was no longer necessary to hold prisoners as an example to others.[148]

One of the soldiers from the 620th summed up the sentiments of the men in camp: "We hadn't anticipated things coming out the way they did. We got the wrong kind of publicity."[149] After the war, Camp Hale shut down operations. It served as a government training center from 1956 to 1965, when the government deactivated the camp and turned the land over to the U.S. Forest Service. In 1992, it was placed on the National Register of Historic Places.

# Notes

GCM: General court-martial of Dale Maple. Those records are preserved in five volumes (files) by the National Archives.
FF: Folder files from the History Colorado Center.

## Chapter 1

1. Dale H. Maple's middle initial didn't stand for anything. He stopped using the middle initial after college. His mother claimed membership in the Daughters of the American Revolution.
2. John Felker letter November 10, 1948, FF 40; Dale H. Maple, home address: Paradise Apartments, Prospect Avenue, Middletown, RI, Dunster House, Glee Club, Comparative Philology, intended vocation: teaching, Harvard yearbook, www.e-yearbook.com.
3. GCM, Volume 3.
4. *Time*, October 28, 1940, 48; GCM, Volume 2. Maple later testified the bust of Hitler was given to him in the summer of 1940 by a fellow student. He said he destroyed it "after that episode had taken some unfortunate turns."
5. FF 1569.
6. Remini, *History of the House of Representatives*, 322. See also Stone, *Perilous Times*, 245–47, 354.
7. GCM, Volume 3, Psychiatric summary of March 4, 1944, by Dr. Blackman.
8. Ibid., Volume 2.

9. Ibid., Volume 1, JAG Opinion of the Board of Review, June 22, 1944.
10. Ibid.; GCM, Volume 2, Report of Psychologist, March 10, 1944. A psychologist named Captain William Gray noted that Maple knew forty-one words of the vocabulary section of the Stanford-Binet Test. Getting thirty right was enough for the "Superior Adult III" category.
11. GCM, Volume 2.
12. FF 1569.
13. Ibid. Maple's childhood piano teacher was Paul Maiss. Maple often performed at the El Cortez Hotel: "Polonaise Militaire"and "Fantaisie" by Chopin, "Polichinelle" by Rachmaninoff, "Allegro Barbaro" by Bartok, and "Concert Etude" by MacDowell.
14. *Chicago Tribune*, September 8, 1935.
15. *San Bernardino News*, July 21, 1915.
16. Jack Williams, obituary, *Union-Tribune*, March 9, 1999.
17. FF 42.
18. Ibid., 1569.
19. Ibid.
20. Ibid., 42.
21. Ibid., 1569.
22. GCM., Volume 4, Memorandum for the Officer in Charge, February 25, 1944.
23. Ibid., Volume 5, Preliminary Report of Investigation, March 10, 1944.
24. FF 56, 4820; FF 42; GCM, Volume 2.
25. Lee, *Fort Meade & The Black Hills*, 228. Prisoners of war did end up at Fort Meade but not until November 1944.
26. FF 55.
27. Remini, *History of the House of Representatives*, 326–29. The Selective Service Act, passed by Congress in the summer of 1940 at the president's request, required men from twenty-one to thirty-five years of age to register for a one-year training period. This law, the first peacetime draft in American history, came up for renewal in Congress a year later. The president requested an indefinite extension "until such time as may be necessary in the interests of national defense." Four months before Pearl Harbor, the House of Representatives decided by 1 vote, 203 to 202, to extend the draft for eighteen more months.
28. FF 1569; GCM, Volume 3.
29. GCM, Volume 5.
30. Ibid.
31. FF 55. A few years later, in March 1950, a woman who had heard about Maple—"that Nazi"—when he was at Harvard wrote to E.J. Kahn that she

assumed soldiers like Maple would be placed "a safe distance from anywhere he could put his ideas into practice. Perhaps in the wilds of some Pacific island or peeling potatoes in the Aleutians, but certainly far, far away from his beloved Germans." The woman attended Radcliffe at the same time Maple was at Harvard, but she heard about him from his fellow classmates.

32. FF 42.
33. Letter from Orson P. Jones, GCM, Volume 6.
34. GCM, Volume 2.
35. Representative Tom Pickett letter, GCM, Volume 1, February 17, 1950.
36. GCM, Volume 5.
37. Ibid., Volume 1; Smart and Smart, *Introduction to Family Relationships*, 21–22.
38. The research project was authored by Nadine Lambert and published by the California State Department of Education.
39. GCM, Volume 2.
40. Ibid., psychiatrist report, March 13, 1944.
41. Ibid., Volume 1; FF 56.
42. Executive Office for the U.S. Attorneys, *Bicentennial Celebration*. Howard F. Houk served as U.S. district attorney for New Mexico from 1942 to 1946. The Department of Justice later dropped the word *district* from the title.
43. *Time*, March 6, 1944, 70.
44. *Rocky Mountain News*, February 20, 1944; FF 42.

## Chapter 2

45. GCM, Volume 4, Preliminary Report of Investigation, March 10, 1944, 4.
46. Koop, *Stark Decency*, 49, 51.
47. Ibid., 59.
48. Hurt, *Great Plains During World War II*.
49. Krammer, *Nazi Prisoners of War*, 120.
50. Ibid., 129–39.
51. Lewis and Mewha, *History of Prisoner of War Utilization*, 83, 90.
52. Cook, *Guests Behind the Barbed Wire*, 25–27.
53. Lewis and Mewha, *History of Prisoner of War Utilization*, 81, 89; Thompson, *Men in German Uniform*.
54. Lewis and Mewha, *History of Prisoner of War Utilization*, 127.
55. Fiedler, *Enemy Among Us*; Krammer, *Nazi Prisoners of War*, 107.
56. Lewis and Mewha, *History of Prisoner of War Utilization*, 263.
57. Reiss, "Bronzed Bodies Behind Barbed Wire," 475.

58. Herman and Jones, "Fairfax Camp," 5–14; Holl, "Axis Prisoners of War," 145.
59. *Chillicothe Tribune*, June 8, 1948; *Warren Times Mirror*, March 4, 1948; *Rhinelander Daily News*, February 28, 1948.
60. *Chillicothe Tribune*, June 8, 1948; *Warren Times Mirror*, March 4, 1948; *Rhinelander Daily News*, February 28, 1948.
61. *Lead (SD) Daily Caller*, January 25, 1948; *Buffalo Courier-Express*, January 25, 1948.
62. *Lebanon Daily News*, November 16, 1945.
63. *Fitchburg Sentinel*, January 23, 1946; November 10 and 13, 1945; Krammer, *Nazi Prisoners of War*, 129. The *Fitchburg Sentinel* found the need to include in its article that she was "squat, bespectacled and unglamorous."
64. *Las Cruces Sun News*, December 26, 1946.
65. FBI annual reports, viewed at www.hathitrust.org.
66. FF 1569.
67. Lewis and Mewha, *History of Prisoner of War Utilization*, 88.
68. Carlson, *We Were Each Other's Prisoners*, 153.
69. Ibid., 209.
70. Thompson, *Men in German Uniform*, 31–32.
71. Krammer, *Nazi Prisoners of War*, 51.
72. Koop, *Stark Decency*, 24.
73. Thompson, *Men in German Uniform*, 59; F.G. Alletson Cook, *New York Times*, November 21, 1943.
74. Thompson, *German Jackboots*, 83.
75. Hamann, *On American Soil*, 53.
76. Ibid.
77. Ibid.
78. Fiedler, *Enemy Among Us*, 395.
79. Cook, *Guests Behind the Barbed Wire*, 502.
80. Whittingham, *Martial Justice*. The POWs had murdered POW Johannes Kunz in November 1943 at the Tonkawa, Oklahoma branch camp.

## Chapter 3

81. GCM, Volume 4.
82. GCM, Volume 2. The gun, a Colt revolver, serial number 8525, blue steel, short barrel, was purchased for $32.50 at M&M Company in Denver. The morning report of February 15, 1944, filed by First Lieutenant Leroy Wilson showed Maple AWOL as of 0800. The Reo automobile was a four-door

sedan, license plate 31-207. The women's clothes purchased for the trip to Germany (via Mexico) included a red-flowered crepe scarf ($1.00), a sport pocket-book ($1.00) and a canary-yellow sweater ($3.95). The items were purchased at the Crews-Beggs Mercantile Company.

83. GCM, Volume 2; GCM, Volume 4, in Captain John M. Curran's Report, March 15, 1944.

## CHAPTER 4

84. *Life Magazine*, November 12, 1945.

85. *Picture Post*, March 2, 1946.

86. FBI personnel records. Bryce had two tattoos on his arms: a horsefly on his right and one with a cross and heart and the word *Mother* on the left. He was divorced in 1932 on the grounds of neglect and adultery. As of 1934, he was paying $40 per month in alimony for the support of a minor child. When hired by the FBI, Bryce's salary was $2,900. In December 1935, Hoover blasted Bryce for negligence and lack of judgment in the unsatisfactory and inefficient manner in which Bryce mishandled surveillance in Bagley, Minnesota. As a result, Hoover canceled a scheduled promotion for Bryce and instead demoted Bryce, whose salary went from $3,200 to $3,000. But from then on, Bryce's career took off. Glowing letters from Hoover fill Bryce's FBI personnel file. In January 1943, Bryce received a promotion to $5,800 (from $5,600) for outstanding work in espionage and sabotage cases. Bryce often received commendations from Hoover for his exemplary fashion and excellent manner for everything from apprehending and interrogating fugitives, putting on firearm exhibits, and writing letters to newspapers rebutting unfavorable editorials about Hoover and the FBI, clarifying the facts one might say.

87. GCM, Volume 4, Memorandum for the Officer in Charge, February 25, 1944.

88. Ibid.

89. U.S. Army, *Manual for Courts-Martial*, 218, 222.

90. GCM, Volume 2. Members of the court-martial panel were Major General Walter E. Prosser, Brigadier General Creswell Garlington, Colonel Ernest J. Carr, Colonel William R. Irvin, Colonel Lawrence L. Conrad, Colonel Richard E. Anderson (scheduled to be in court but excused by verbal orders of Major General Danielson), Colonel Barndt A. Anderson, Colonel Vernon L. Padgett, Colonel Arthur C. Blain,

Lieutenant Colonel Courtney P. Young (who made a point to say he had read the *Time* magazine excerpt, but he was not prejudiced and had not formed an opinion), Lieutenant Colonel Clarence Frankforter, Lieutenant Colonel George W. Prichard (law member), Captain Bernard F. Ladon (trial judge advocate) and Second Lieutenant Clarence E. Vores (assistant trial judge advocate). The defense counsel were Humphrey Biddle of Biddle and Biddle Law Firm, Leavenworth, Kansas; Lieutenant William Fleischaker; and Major Rinold L. Ohman. Colonel Hosterman, Colonel White, Colonel Reed and Captain Perry DeWalt attended as observers.

91. Ibid.
92. Ibid.
93. Ibid.
94. GCM, Volume 1, Opinion of the Board of Review, June 22, 1944; GCM, Volume 6, Major General C.H. Danielson, Memorandum of March 14, 1944.
95. GCM, Volumes 1 and 6; Lipps court-martial (CM) file.
96. GCM, Volume 1, Hubert D. Hoover memo, March 17, 1949 (items 10, 11, 12); U.S. Army, *North African Theatre Operations*; Weyl, *Treason*, 342–47; FF 1569; Burton and Green, "Defining Disloyalty," 215.
97. Weyl, *Treason*, 392–96; FF 1569.
98. Dale Lipps was inducted in the army on November 17, 1941, and assigned to Company C, 389th Battalion. He faced a general court-martial, which convened on April 19, 1944. He was convicted and sentenced to a ten-year confinement at the Disciplinary Barracks, Greenhaven, New York.

## Chapter 5

99. GCM, Volume 2.
100. Ibid.
101. Ibid.
102. Ibid.
103. Ibid., Volume 4.
104. Ibid., Volume 5.
105. Kahn, E.J. "Who Wants to Go to Germany in Wartime?" *New Yorker*, April 1, 1950, 68.
106. GCM, Volume 4.
107. FF 56.
108. GCM, Volume 4.
109. Siering CM.

110. Ibid.
111. FF 56.
112. Siering CM; FF 56.
113. GCM, Volume 2.
114. The psychiatrists were First Lieutenant Sylvan Solarz, Major Thomas Metzgar, Captain Ervin Chappell, Captain Nathan Blackman, Colonel Edward Strickler, Captain Edward Powell. In Albuquerque, at the behest of District Attorney Houk and Agent Bryce, Dr. Stewart examined Maple.
115. GCM, Volume 1, Opinion of the Board of Review, June 22, 1944.
116. Ibid., Volume 3, Psychiatric summary, March 4, 1944 by Dr. Blackman.
117. Ibid., Volume 2.
118. Ibid.
119. Ibid.
120. Ibid.
121. Ibid., Volume 1, Opinion of the Board of Review, June 22, 1944.
122. GCM, Volume 1, War Department Report, May 21, 1944.
123. Ibid., Volume 1.
124. Ibid., War Department Report, May 21, 1944.
125. U.S. House of Representatives, *Investigations of the National War Effort*, 22–23.
126. *Rocky Mountain News*, March 10, 1944; *Troy Record*, March 19, 1944; Major Carl D. Ganz, report dated March 10, 1944; Kahn, "Philologist"; newspaper articles posted on the Metropolitan State College of Denver's website, www.mscd.edu/~history/camphale. Frederick Maurer stated he had been to the Rim Rock Lodge once, and there was a WAC there at the time, someone whom they called "Scotty" (GCM, Volume 5). Schwichtenberg boasted the WACS would bring him whatever he wanted (Siering court-martial file, p. 10).

# CHAPTER 6

127. FF 1569. Per the *Biographical Directory of the American Congress*, Porter (April 4, 1919–January 1, 2006) graduated from Harvard in 1941 and Harvard Law School in 1947. He served overseas in England, France, Belgium, Luxembourg and Czechoslovakia during World War II and was awarded four battle stars and a distinguished unit citation. He was a law clerk in 1947 and 1948 in the U.S. Court of Appeals in San Francisco and admitted to the bar in 1948.

128. FF 1569.
129. FF 49.
130. Ibid.
131. Ibid.
132. "The Philologist," by E.J. Kahn, was published in four separate *New Yorker* issues in 1950: "A Trip to Old Palomas" on March 11, "Dissonance in the Tower" on March 18, "A State of Agitation" on March 25, and "Who Wants to Go to Germany in Wartime?" on April 1.
133. FF 40, 42, 1569. The award was called the Wayne Gridley Award. Nothing appeared on Google for Wayne Gridley, and the author's contact with the San Diego Alumni Association had no knowledge of the name or the award.

## Epilogue

134. GCM, Volume 2.
135. The name of the case was East Coast Tender Service Inc. v Robert T. Winzinger Inc., 759 F.2d 280.
136. Larry Pearson, *Rocky Mountain News*, June 7, 1964, 22.
137. FF 55.
138. FF 42.
139. FF 56.
140. Hotelling's testimony was before the U.S. Senate, Committee on Nutrition and Human Needs.
141. FF 1569.
142. Moore, *Wacko War*, 59–60.
143. *Biographical Directory of the American Congress*; Moore, *Wacko War*, 60–63.
144. FBI Annual Reports FY 1944 and 1945; Lewis and Mewha, *History of Prisoner of War Utilization.*
145. Cook, *Guests Behind the Barbed Wire*, 462, 485, 492; Lewis and Mewha, *History of Prisoner of War Utilization*, 173.
146. Waters, *Lone Star Stalag*, 145.
147. U.S. House of Representatives, *Investigations of the National War Effort.*
148. FF 1569.
149. Ibid.

# Bibliography


Benice, Ronald J. "Florida Prisoner of War Scrip." *Paper Money*, January/February 2012: 73.

Billinger, Robert, Jr. *Hitler's Soldiers in the Sunshine State*. Gainesville: University Press of Florida, 2000.

———. *Nazi POWs in the Tar Heel State*. Gainesville: University Press of Florida, 2008.

*Biographical Directory of the American Congress*. Washington D.C.: U.S. Government Printing Office, 1971.

Burton, Shirley, and Kellee Green. "Defining Disloyalty: Treason, Espionage, and Sedition Prosecutions, 1861–1946." *Prologue* 21, no. 3 (Fall 1989): 215.

Carlson, Lewis H. *We Were Each Other's Prisoners: An Oral History of World War II American and German Prisoners of War*. New York: Basic Books, 1997.

*Chicago Tribune*, September 8, 1935.

Conti, Mike. *Jelly Bryce: FBI Odyssey, A Novel*. North Reading, MA: Saber Press, 2015.

Cook, Ruth Beaumont. *Guests Behind the Barbed Wire: German POWs in America; A True Story of Hope and Friendship*. Birmingham, AL: Crane Hill Publishers, 2006.

Cowley, Betty. *Stalag Wisconsin: Inside WWII Prisoner of War Camps*. Oregon, WI: Badger Books, 2002.

Culley, John Joel. "A Troublesome Presence: World War II Internment of German Sailors in New Mexico." *Prologue* 28, No. 4 (Winter 1996): 279.

Executive Office for the U.S. Attorneys. Bicentennial Celebration of the United States Attorneys, 1789–1989.

Fay, Sidney B. "German Prisoners of War." *Monthly Magazine of World Affairs* 8, no. 43 (March 1945): 193.

Federal Bureau of Investigation: Annual Reports, FY 1944 and 1945. Viewed at www.hathitrust.org.

Fiedler, David. *The Enemy Among Us: POWs in Missouri During World War II*. St. Louis: Missouri Historical Society Press, 2003.

Hamann, Jack. *On American Soil: How Justice Became a Casualty of World War II*. Chapel Hill, NC: Algonquin Books, 2005.

Herbert, Paul N. *God Knows All Your Names: Obscure Stories in American History*. Bloomington, IN: Author House Publishing, 2009.

Herman, Adam, and Christopher F. Jones. "The Fairfax Camp: German Prisoners of War in Fairfax County During World War II." *Yearbook, The Historical Society of Fairfax County, Virginia* 23: 5–14.

Higbee, Paul. "Suspects in Sturgis." *South Dakota Magazine*, November/December 2000: 47.

Holian, Timothy J. *The German-Americans and World War II: An Ethnic Experience*. New York: Peter Lang Publishing, 1996.

Holl, Richard E. "Axis Prisoners of War in the Free State, 1943–1946." *Maryland Historical Magazine* 83, no. 2 (Summer 1988): 142.

Hurt, R. Douglas. *The Great Plains During World War II*. Lincoln: University of Nebraska Press, 2008.

Kahn, E.J., "The Philologist." 4 parts. *New Yorker*, March 11, March 18, March 25, and April 1, 1950.

Koop, Allen V. *Stark Decency: German Prisoners of War in a New England Village*. Lebanon, NH: University Press of New England, 1988.

Krammer, Arnold. *Nazi Prisoners of War in America*. Lanham, MD: Scarborough House Publishers, 1979.

Lambert, Nadine. "The Emotionally Handicapped Child and the School: A Research Program in the Prevention of Personality and Behavior Disorders in Children." Sacramento: California State Department of Education, 1959.

Lee, Robert. *Fort Meade & The Black Hills*. Lincoln: University of Nebraska Press, 1991.

Lentz-Adams, Meredith. *Murder and Martial Justice: Spying and Retribution in World War II America*. Kent, OH: Kent State University Press, 2011.

Lewis, Lieutenant Colonel George G., and Captain John Mewha. *History of Prisoner of War Utilization by the United States Army 1776–1945*. Department of the Army Pamphlet, Number 20-213, June 1955. Viewed at Hathitrust.org.

*Life Magazine*, November 12, 1945.

Luick-Thrams, Michael. *Held in the Heartland: German POWs in the Midwest, 1943–1946*. Pamphlet, BUS-eum, 2008.

Mallett, Derek R. *Hitler's Generals in America: Nazi POWs and Allied Military Intelligence*. Lexington: University of Kentucky Press, 2013.

Marsh, Melissa Amateis. *Nebraska POW Camps: A History of World War II Prisoners in the Heartland*. Charleston, SC: The History Press, 2014.

Marshall, David. *San Diego's Balboa Park*. Charleston, SC: Arcadia Publishing, 2007.

Metropolitan State College of Denver. www.mscd.edu/~history/camphale.

Moore, John Hammond. *The Faustball Tunnel: German POWs in America and Their Great Escape*. New York: Random House, 1978.

———. *Wacko War: Strange Tales from America, 1941–1945*. Bur Oak Circle, NC: Pentland Press, 2001.

Owens, Ron. *Legendary Lawman: The Story of Quick Draw Jelly Bryce*. Nashville, TN: Turner Publishing Company, 2010.

*Picture Post*, March 2, 1946.

Reiss, Matthias. "Bronzed Bodies Behind Barbed Wire: Masculinity and the Treatment of German Prisoners of War in the United States During World War II." *Journal of Military History* 69, no. 2 (April 2005): 475.

Remini, Robert V. *The History of the House of Representatives*. Washington, D.C.: Smithsonian Books, in association with HarperCollins Publishers, 2006.

Robin, Ron. *The Barbed Wire College: Re-educating German POWs in the United States During World War II*. Princeton, NJ: Princeton University Press, 1995.

*Rocky Mountain News*, February 20, 1944.

*San Bernardino News*, July 21, 1915.

*San Diego Union-Tribune*, March 9, 1999.

Schmitter Heisler, Barbara. *From German Prisoner of War to American Citizen: A Social History with 35 Interviews*. Jefferson, NC: McFarland & Company, Inc., 2013.

Smart, Mollie, and Russell Smart. *An Introduction to Family Relationships*. Philadelphia: Saunders, 1953.

Stone, Geoffrey R. *Perilous Times, Free Speech in Wartime: From the Sedition Act of 1798 to the War on Terrorism*. New York: W.W. Norton, 2004.

Thompson, Antonio S. *German Jackboots on Kentucky Bluegrass: Housing German Prisoners of War in Kentucky, 1942–1946*. Clarksville, TN: Diversion Press, 2008.

———. *Men in German Uniform: POWs in America During World War II*. Knoxville: University of Tennessee Press, 2010.

*Time*, October 28, 1940; March 6, 1944.

U.S. Army. Files pertaining to the courts-martial of Dale Maple, Frederick Siering, Dale Lipps, Fritz Loock. Obtained from the National Archives through a Freedom of Information Act Request.

———. *A Manual for Courts-Martial, U.S. Army, 1928 (Corrected to April 20, 1943).* Washington, D.C.: Government Printing Office, 1943.

———. *North African Theatre of Operations and Mediterranean Theatre of Operations, Board of Review Opinions, 1944.* Washington, D.C.: Office of the Judge Advocate General, 1945. Viewed at https://loc.gov/rr/frd/Military_Law/pdf/ETO-BOR_Vol-4.pdf.

U.S. House of Representatives. *Investigation of the National War Effort: Report of the Committee on Military Affairs.* June 1946.

U.S. Office of Personnel Management (OPM). FBI personnel records of Delf A. Bryce. Records obtained through the Freedom of Information Act.

Waters, Michael R. *Lone Star Stalag: German Prisoners of War at Camp Hearne.* College Station: Texas A&M University Press, 2004.

Weyl, Nathaniel. *Treason: The Story of Disloyalty and Betrayal in American History.* Washington, D.C.: Public Affairs Press, 1950.

Whittingham, Richard. *Martial Justice: The Last Mass Execution in the United States.* Claremore, OK: Country Lane Press, 1988.

# About the Author

*At about noon the next day, February 19, 1944, at the Doña Ana County Jail in Las Cruces, New Mexico, a legendary lawman nicknamed "Jellybean" interviewed the disheveled itinerant named Müeller. Here fame collided with infamy, renown with notoriety; the man on one side of the desk would later have books written about him and be featured in* Life Magazine, *the other in* Time.

So writes award-winning historian Paul N. Herbert as he once again narrates a true story touching on emotions of fear, disloyalty and trust. Herbert masterfully paints the milieu during World War II in the Rockies, where the path of a Harvard University graduate intersected with those of prisoners of war to form a most intriguing story, one never told in book form. Join Herbert as he connects the dots of history to make nonfiction read like fiction, compelling readers to try to determine whether history really repeats itself. History doesn't get any more fascinating or obscure than this.

Paul N. Herbert has had numerous articles published in newspapers and magazines and his books include *The Jefferson Hotel: The History of a Richmond Landmark* and *Elinor Fry: A Legacy of Dance in Richmond*. He lives in Virginia and can be contacted at treasonintherockies@yahoo.com.

*Visit us at*
www.historypress.net

*This title is also available as an e-book*